One World
A Progressive Vision for Enforceable Global Law
Democracy

One World
A Progressive Vision for Enforceable Global Law
Democracy

Jerry Tetalman and **Byron Belitsos**

Origin Press

San Rafael, California

Origin Press

P.O. Box 151117, San Rafael, CA 94915
www.OriginPress.com

Cover and book design by Phillip Dizick
pdizick@earthlink.net

Publisher's Cataloging-in-Publication
(Provided by Quality Books, Inc.)

Tetalman, Jerry.
    One world democracy : a progressive vision for
enforceable global law / by Jerry Tetalman and Byron
Belitsos.
    p. cm.
    Includes bibliographical references.
    LCCN 2005925238
    ISBN 978-1-57983-017-5
    ISBN 1-57983-017-X

    1. International organization. 2. International
relations. 3. Democratization. 4. Rule of law.
I. Belitsos, Byron, 1953- II. Title.

JZ5566.4.T48 2005   341.2'1
                                 QBI05-600045

First printing: June 2005
10 9 8 7 6 5 4 3 2 1

PRINTED IN THE UNITED STATES OF AMERICA ON RECYCLED PAPER

This book is dedicated
to all those who are working for
peace, justice, and sustainability—
now and into the far future.

Acknowledgements

My wife for the gift of encouragement.
My daughter for the gift of belief.
My mother for the gift of thinking big.
My brother and sisters for the gift of staying balanced.
Melvin Clay for the gift of independent thinking.
Lynn Sparks for the gift of non-conformity.
Jessica Clark for the gift of teaching writing.
Carrie Cantor for the gift of organization.
Judy Cullins for the gift of just going for it.
Jane Shevtsov for the gift of understanding.
Mike, Matt and Tom Ferry for the gift of self-confidence.
Jim Van Der Water for the gift of taking action.
Ann Hoiberg for the gift of helping.
Byron Belitsos for the gift of teamwork.
Donna Volpe for the gift of courage.
Garry Davis for the gift of activism.
George Marsh for the gift of saying what you mean.
Phillip Dizick for the gift of being an artist.
Gwen Price for the gift of precision.
Lauren Dowell for the gift of kindness.
Zadi Balouch for the gift of loyalty.
Robin Ardez for the gift of planning.
Ed Duliba for the gift of dedication.
Aaron Knight for the gift leadership.
Therese Tanalski for the gift of having a cause.
Bill Bryant for the gift of support.
John Sutter for the gift of connecting people.
Antera for the gift of accomplishment.
Mike Fraijo for the gift of trust.

—**Jerry Tetalman**

I would like to acknowledge my mentors in the world federalist movement, including but not limited to: Tad Daley, Bob Gauntt, and Lucile Green, as well as those who most inspired me: Garry Davis, Troy Davis, Ben Ferencz, Jerry Gerber, Pat Fearey, Roger Kotila, Steve McIntosh, and Chuck Thurston. A special thanks to John Sutter for superb editorial input, and also to the Democratic World Federalists in San Francisco, including Eric Schultz, who over the years have provided the kind of friendship and comradeship that is needed to birth a book like this. Above all, I am grateful to Jerry Tetalman, whose vision, patience, tolerance, and love of humanity made this book possible.

—**Byron Belitsos**

Contents

PART II
Global Problems that Need Global Solutions

PART III
Global Activism for a New Epoch

Preface

We have it in our power to begin the world over again.
—Thomas Paine
Common Sense 1776

This book is an introduction to the greatest political transformation in history—the democratic revolution to create enforceable global law.

This epochal change in human affairs will put an end, once and for all, to the war system that is the greatest scourge facing humankind.

In this revolution, ordinary people will take control of this planet from those who foment war and profit from war, and who permit environmental destruction.

This will be a movement of optimists and visionaries, those who are ready to seize the opportunity to reinvent our world, ready to leave behind the cynics whose only contribution is to maintain the status quo.

In this movement, world peace is not a vague and utopian goal—but a practical, enduring peace that is achieved through world laws that are passed by a democratic world legislature, interpreted by world courts, and enforced by a global government that represents all of humanity, high and low, north and south, black and white.

We truly can create "the parliament of the world, the government of mankind" as the English poet Tennyson prophetically envisioned in the nineteenth century. The time for this historic task is upon us, now, in the twenty-first century.

This global peace and justice movement is already well under way. Worldwide demonstrations like the historic "global day of protest" against the US invasion of Iraq on February 15, 2003 are just one sign.

Yet something more than rejectionism is needed from our progressive leaders. These times require a positive and practical vision for how to solve international conflicts; how to relieve global poverty; and how to end the physical destruction of our precious planet.

We therefore ask you to imagine a world peace movement focused on making the United Nations, or some successor, into a *truly representative government for all humanity.*

Imagine a global legislature or world parliament whose first order of business is the abolition of war.

Envision a world court whose routine work is to apply global law to individuals, rather than punishing entire nations for the crimes of their leaders.

Visualize a planetary bill of rights that is zealously guarded, and a constitutional balance of power that prevents excesses by any branch of the world government.

Reflect on the satisfaction of living peacefully under the rule of global law where there is *less* government, *lower* taxes, *better* distribution of resources, *no* nuclear weapons, *open* borders, *less* environmental destruction, *no* imperial domination, *no* military-industrial complex, *more* security, *more* justice for labor and minorities—and a global renaissance in the arts, science, religion, and culture.

And imagine yourself a part of this, the greatest political movement ever to occur.

We the people of planet earth are the sovereigns of our destiny; if we stand together, we can build a just and democratic government of humankind that will abolish war forever, and work together with all nations to solve the other pressing problems facing our fragile planet. It really can be that simple—and that exhilarating.

This book is directed especially at progressives and visionary leaders in all walks of life who care deeply about global justice, reduction of poverty worldwide, and the protection of the planet's environment—but especially those who are working for world peace.

In our view, today's world peace movement is too often marked by a naive utopianism that confuses human nature with angelic nature. Angels can live in peace without law and government—but humans cannot. In our all-too-human world, peace without justice is an illusion—an uneasy truce until the next war comes along, such as the intractable Israeli-Palestinian conflict. Global justice, we argue, is simply not achievable without the establishment of law by an elected legislature in combination with judicial institutions that interpret and apply the law. And courts of law are almost useless without enforcement mechanisms—the notorious impotence of the UN being a case in point. Those who aspire for world peace really have no choice but to work for the achievement of enforceable global law.

"There is no peace without justice, no justice without law, and no law without government"—according to the formula of the United World Federalists of the late 1940s. The decades since then have only affirmed the truth of this old activist slogan. A great day is coming when the world's peace movement and social justice progressives will once again embrace this crucial syllogism; and that is the day when we will become empowered to end war and ecocide. Only then will there be an end to the military dominance of America and a genuine solution to terrorism. Only then can we really tackle the daunting problems of global pollution and grinding poverty.

Let us use the twenty-first century to create the end of war—not the end of humankind. To abolish war we will need enforceable global law—the expansion of civilization to a planetary scale. This book invites you on a lifelong journey to the achievement of planetary peace and prosperity. Let's get there by working to build one world democracy.

One World
A Progressive Vision for Enforceable Global Law
Democracy

Part I

Principles of Democratic Global Governance

1

The Peoples of the World Are Sovereign

Today we must develop federal structures on a global level. We need a system of enforceable world law—a democratic federal world government—to deal with world problems.
—Walter Cronkite

Imagine an old *Star Trek* series like this: Captain Kirk and crew are out exploring deep space, getting into quirky dramas on far-distant planets; meanwhile, back on earth, Kirk's home planet is a war-torn cauldron of sovereign nation-states armed to the teeth. A dozen wars are going on at any one time, and thousands of children die of starvation daily. Its leading superpower is fighting a global war on terrorists, mounting computerized weapons in space, and standing by while global warming destroys the planet's ecosystem.

Not exactly a suitable home port for a Captain Kirk.

Star Trek instead depicted an "Earth Federation" in our future—an advanced civilization ruled by a democratic global government. Pessimistic science fiction writers usually resort to the flipside scenario, some version of a nightmarish future dystopia in which humankind has failed to rise to the manifold challenges of war, conflict, and greed. They indulge in an imaginative extension of the current planetary anarchy that we read about in the newspaper every day.

Which portrayal will win out? This book is about the proposition that there really *is* no acceptable future without enforceable global laws that will outlaw war, redistribute resources, and control pollution. We will present the vision of a real-life "earth federation," and we believe that today's progressives must lead the worldwide grassroots campaign that will make it come true—before it's too late. But can we dare to imagine a global democratic government evolving, even in our own time? Or must the whole world endure more deadly warfare, terrorism, and ecocide before we come to our senses? Our common foe is the destruction of the planet by the quick method of nuclear war or the slow method of environmental collapse. Let us soberly look to these common threats, and summon the courage to affirm the ideal of uniting all of humanity around a global social contract. It was the great scientist Albert Einstein who wrote: "The UN now, and world government eventually, must serve one single goal—the guarantee of the security, tranquility, and the welfare of all mankind."

The ideal of "one world" was established in the 1940s

The ideal of a united human family began to dawn on masses of people, at least young Americans, in the great activist era of the 1960s. The first pictures of the earth from space were beamed back from the moon in 1969. The Apollo astronauts reported great epiphanies as they viewed the planet from deep space for the first time. The visionaries and antiwar activists of the sixties, and these fortunate astronauts, pictured planet earth as it really is: a unified whole, a global family of humanity, a gorgeous sphere without the artificial borders that can lead to division and war.

Seen from a distance in space or time, our deadly internecine squabbles, our monstrous war system, and our inability to protect the global environment and feed the poor seem backward and childish indeed. In this book we will invite you to step back in your imagination, and envision our planet's true destiny that lies beyond our current nationalistic prejudices—the earth as a politically unified sphere of diverse peoples who live in peace.

This vision of a unified humanity has been growing ever since the 1960s, and in recent years has found remarkable expression in a rugged, worldwide peace and justice movement. This movement comprises a key part of the progressive vanguard of the coming "one world democracy." Probably its greatest public moment was the simultaneous demonstrations on February 15, 2003 in over forty cities worldwide by an estimated 30 million people opposed to the Iraq war.[1] Another key element of this global progressive movement is the annual meetings of the World Social Forum. The WSF was created in 2001 to provide an open platform to discuss strategies of resistance to the prevailing model for globalization that gets presented each year at the annual World Economic Forum at Davos, Switzerland by large multinational corporations, national governments, the IMF (International Monetary Fund), the World Bank, and the WTO.

But as you will see in this book, a crucial element is still missing from these creative and potent expressions of protest and resistance: a positive program to end war and exploitation through enforceable global law and a federation of nations, including a world legislature. We call those activists who susbcribe to this approach "enlightened progressives."

We believe that such a vision of a great global democracy, ruled by just laws and based on the inherent sovereignty of the people of the world, could powerfully unify today's progressive activists. With a clear objective of making war illegal through the rule of enforceable global law, the antiwar movement will grow similar to the way the abolitionist movement grew to eliminate slavery in the US in the nineteenth century.

The roots of this vision are not just a matter of imagination or science fiction. We need only backtrack a few decades from the antiwar movement of the '60s and revisit the "one world" ideals of the postwar generation of the late 1940s.

The narrative of the post-WWII peace movement and its various initiatives for "one world" through world federal government is an inspiring story of noble ideals and courageous leadership. Very few of today's progressive activists are aware that a vibrant world federalist movement dominated the scene in the US in the second half of the 1940s—long before the 1960s. This movement had its beginnings in that unsung generation of activists and thinkers of the post-war era who arose after the nuclear era was suddenly inaugurated in the mushroom ball at Hiroshima. Renowned writers and leaders such as philosopher Mortimer Adler, physicist Albert Einstein, Supreme Court Justice Owen Roberts, presidential candidate Henry Wallace, attorney Grenville Clark, educator Robert Hutchins, and journalist E.B. White led the way and set the tone for thousands of activists.

During that forgotten era, an activist group called the Student Federalists was considered the most progressive. The largest organization, the United World Federalists (UWF), formed in 1947 by the merger of five groups, once had over 50,000 members, with affiliates in almost every state and on scores of campuses. Declining after the disillusionment of the

Korean War, the UWF went through several changes until it reemerged in the 1960s under the leadership of *Saturday Evening Post* editor Norman Cousins. After a period of decline, it was resurrected as the World Federalist Association (WFA) in 1976, and was based for three decades in Washington D.C. The WFA recently changed its name to Citizens for Global Solutions (CGS), with a focus on legislation and UN reform. The formation of CGS left behind several important splinters, most notably the Democratic World Federalists, based in San Francisco, which is a new national organization more specifically dedicated to the goal of world federation. In chapter four we also review two other grassroots movements dedicated to global democracy.

To get a sense of what the earliest blossoming of the "one world" movement was like, here is one vivid story of the progressive activism from that era:

Garry Davis was a young professional actor and a former US air force pilot who had become disillusioned with war after personally participating in the fire-bombing of German civilian targets. Mulling over his war experience one day in late 1948, something profound rose up in him and moved him to act. He pulled together some money and flew to Paris, to the temporary United Nations headquarters then at Palais Chaillot. Appearing outside the palace before the press and a crowd of observers, he dramatically renounced his US citizenship, proclaiming himself a "citizen of the world." His next move was to literally camp just outside the UN head-quarters on a small bit of space that he publicly declared to be "liberated world territory."

Then, with the support of activists whom he had rallied to his cause, Davis conceived of another publicity-grabbing event. One day, he made bold to enter the UN's General Assembly itself. He stood up and interrupted a session to present a dramatic plea for a genuine world government—that is, until he was seized by UN guards. But at that very moment an associate named Robert Sarrazac, a former lieutenant colonel in the French military, arose and finished Davis' speech, saying, "We, the people, long for the peace which only a world order can give. The sovereign states which you represent here are dividing us and bringing us to the abyss of war." Sarrazac called on the astonished delegates to cease their national disputes and "raise a flag around which all men can gather, the flag of sovereignty of one government for the world."

Inspired by Davis' sensational activities, over 250,000 people from many nations registered as "world citizens" through his new organization in the months thereafter; each made their own personal declaration of world citizenship. Meanwhile, approximately 400 cities and towns throughout France, Belgium, Denmark, Germany, and India—in part following Garry Davis' example—proclaimed themselves "mundialized," (or world territory), in the next few years. The so-called mundialization movement, largely symbolic in nature, soon faded in the confusion of the Cold War, but the world citizens' movement had now been launched.[2]

This incident colorfully illustrates the key concepts of sovereignty that underlie this introductory discussion of global government. The issues and questions involved here are profound: What is true sovereignty? Can there be a "flag of sovereignty of one government for the world," as Davis and Sarrazac proclaimed, or was this a fanciful metaphor? Does the evolution of sovereignty end with nation-states? Do individuals have rights only as citizens of nations—but not as citizens of the world? And what would it take to "mundialize" our world once again, only this time for good?

Peace always grows
as sovereignty expands

To get at an answer, we must first ask what sovereignty actually is, and how and from whom it is derived. After the fall of Rome in the West, the term came to refer to the so-called divine right of kings to rule, a right of sovereignty that was believed to be conferred on the throne directly by God.

A great landmark was reached when King John of England was compelled to sign the Magna Carta in 1215, which established in principle that the king was not above the law, and that noblemen and ordinary Englishmen have distinct rights. Beginning in the sixteenth century in Europe, Renaissance and then Enlightenment thinkers began to demolish the intellectual foundations of the feudal concept of divine right. They reasoned that the source of sovereignty must ultimately derive from the *people* over whom kings once ruled, rather than being a set of rights conferred upon the people by the king.

Later theorists have held that sovereignty is inherent and inalienable in individual persons, and cannot as such be transferred to governments. They have argued that the people simply grant "powers of governing" to different levels of government when it is legitimate, or that dictators may temporarily usurp people's innate sovereignty when government is illegitimate.

Generally speaking, all of these writers and legislators have established the enduring democratic truth that sovereignty resides both in individual citizens and in the collective whole of all the people. And thus began the transfer of the power to rule from one person (or one class or one race) to all the people, and the simultaneous recognition that each citizen has the right to "life, liberty, and property"—not just the king, or the nobles, or the ruling classes. This earth-shaking conception of democracy soon became the motivating force that drove the American and French revolutions, inexorably leading humanity to the era of the modern democratic state. Democracy has expanded from these roots in Europe and the US and is now practiced in some form in over one hundred and twenty countries worldwide.

Here is our point: If sovereignty has its source in the people, and if the world has progressively moved in the direction of increasing democracy in recognition of that fact, then this concept must have an even greater destiny than we see today.

History records the fact that the definition of sovereignty has been broadening to encompass ever-larger concepts of human community—ever-more inclusive definitions of who "the people" are. Each such expansion—where limited by constitutional government—has brought peace and security and advances in human rights and liberty to more and more people.

In the most general sense, the evolution of sovereignty can be said to have begun with the primitive family; this was followed by consanguineous (blood-related) clans and tribes. Next came city-states and then warring city-states, such as ancient Greece during its fabled wars between Athens and Sparta, or China before it was unified in the Han Empire.

Much like the Han emperors in the East—and around the same period in world history—the Romans greatly extended sovereignty in the West. Rome enjoyed an unprecedented era of peace known as *Pax Romana* (Roman Peace) that lasted from just before the time of Christ through the fourth century, by incorporating once-sovereign and warring cities and states around the Mediterranean into an integrated whole. The Han Empire, as well as the later Tang and Ming periods in China, were also golden ages of high culture and civil peace. These blessings were conferred upon these peoples through the broadening of the sovereignty of the Chinese state over large regions.

History describes the ways in which the broad reach of these ancient empires did at times break down, causing retrogressions to intervening eras of warring states; this was witnessed after the fall of the Roman Empire as Europe fragmented into hundreds of warring sovereign entities in the "dark ages." Similarly, after its own golden era of several centuries, the fall of the feudal Ottoman Empire in the nineteenth century led to the fragmentation of the Arab world that we see today.

Europe fared far better than the Islamic world in the transition to modern forms of sovereignty and democracy. The intervening era in Europe between feudal empire and modernity witnessed the slow formation of functionally sovereign nations. In the early modern era in the West, the first nation-states arose out of the warring feudal estates of medieval Europe, some later to become sea-faring empires. The Treaty of Westphalia of 1648 enshrined the concept of sovereign nation-states in Europe. Ever since this treaty, the general goal of war and diplomacy has been a "balance of power."

Notable in this evolution were the formation of the United Kingdom, France, Germany, and Italy—Europe's great nations to this day. The frequently warring provinces of Burgundy, Brittany, and Normandy consolidated to form the nation of France in the fifteenth century. James I united

Scotland and England early in the seventeenth century, ending centuries of egregious violence. The unification of Germany and Italy came much later. Europe has lapsed into continent-wide wars many times in the last few millennia, only to overcome this curse with the great success of the European Union (EU) that was effected in the late twentieth century. This political union of Europe is a regional democratic federation of nations that, perhaps more than anything else, presages the world federation to come.

Without exception, all such instances of the broadening and sharing of sovereignty have resulted in peace within the larger sovereign unit; retrogressions have usually led right back to outbreaks of fratricidal conflict.

Peace through broader sovereignty was also in evidence when the early Americans rejected their *confederation* of thirteen states—each with its own militia and sovereign power—and adopted a *federation* of states with a constitution that transferred the right to make war to a national federal government. The colonies won their independence from Britain in 1783, but struggled for five more years as a confederation of states in which each state retained sovereignty. Pennsylvania and Connecticut almost went to war over the treatment of Connecticut citizens who had settled in Pennsylvania. New York and New Jersey exchanged canon fire in New York Harbor over the issue of who would collect taxes from incoming boats. It was not until 1788, after the federal constitution was ratified, that the US was able to become the country we know it to be today, with the first Congress and President seated in 1789.

This act of federal union that led to the United States of America, and more recently the federation of the states of Europe that led to the EU, provide the best modern examples of how a people's decision to grant governing and law-making powers to larger and larger political entities confers the blessings of peace, law, and democracy to a wider territory. Europe, through the recent development of supranational law, has finally found peace after having been a killing field for centuries. Some thirty other countries around the world are based on some form of federations as well.

We've noted that sovereignty can be transferred not only upward but also downward, resulting in a new cycle of wars or the threat of war. In the US, this occurred in the American Civil War, a breakdown of national sovereignty that created two warring "sovereign" units. Something equally deadly occurred in the former Yugoslavia when its socialist federation was broken up into the smaller warring countries of Serbia/Montenegro, Croatia, Slovenia, Bosnia-Herzegovina, and Macedonia, and later Kosovo.

History teaches that any political union can be challenged even after it has become well established; as with any government, a global government will require the continued vigilance of its members and of a vigorous world press if it is to endure and remain free of corruption.

The UN does not represent the sovereignty of humankind

We've seen that, throughout human history, sovereignty has been broadening to encompass an increasingly larger concept of community. We know that this increase in the recognition of the innate sovereign power of the people—based on the inalienable rights of individual citizens—has resulted in peace within the new and larger sovereign unit, and that this broader peace is maintained just to the extent that the rule of law and justice is maintained in that sovereign entity.

The United Nations, of course, does not supply this wider recognition of sovereignty and law; it is not a true sovereign union. We can say categorically that the UN has failed to bring the peace and stability that the broadening of sovereignty has been shown to confer upon humankind.

The UN is a relic of the post-WWII era, hindered in its work by a design similar to that of the failed American confederation of states, which preceded the federal constitution of the US. Under the UN Charter, the right to make war is retained by individual nations; all actions are voluntary; and those agreements approved in the UN Security Council that are not vetoed by one of the five great powers are virtually unenforceable. A global arms race, dozens of bloody wars, and increasing global pollution mark the era of the confederation of nations known as the United Nations. Further, individual rights as such have no standing before the United Nations. Neither the innate sovereignty of the world's people, nor the inherent human rights of persons, are reliably protected by the United Nations charter.

War and anarchy can be eliminated only when a new sovereign source of law is set up over and above the old clashing groups, creating an integrated whole and a higher source of law. The UN is not such a source of supranational law. The UN created a community of nations, and acts on the world stage as an agent for member nations.

But the challenge of our time is the quest to redefine our community as *all of humanity.* We currently see ourselves as Americans, Russians, or Chinese, but are we not truly one human community? Are we not unified by a common source, by the earth we all share, and by the desire for security and peace equally held by people all over the world? Global survival requires that we expand our loyalty to include not just our family, city, state or province, and country, but to humanity and the planet as well—and that we affirm this with global law and democratic governance.

Our loyalty seems to have stopped with the nation, but *competitive nationalism is the greatest barrier to redefining our community as all humanity.* Internally, nationalism is not necessarily an evil; it has been a unifying factor in many countries. But how long can humankind continue as two hundred separate countries, with two hundred armies engaged in an arms race? If nationhood continues to be the reigning form of sovereignty on this planet—and is kept in place through the legitimizing vehicle of the UN—then our future prospects are indeed stark.

It is often said that global government is overly idealistic and not a realistic solution to today's problems. But it seems to us that the real dreamers are those who believe that today's anarchic system of nationalism and war will bring a lasting peace. Anyone who thinks we can find peace by building more weapons of mass destruction (WMDs) should think again. Anyone who argues that the US can create security with a massive Pentagon budget need only bring to mind the scene of the Pentagon itself suffering a withering attack by a few clever terrorists. Those dreamers who think that peace results from an endless arms race will eventually return to square one: History proves over and over again that peace prevails only under the rule of government.

There is much to consider here. Many nations have built or can build weapons of mass destruction. This knowledge cannot be somehow erased by attacking these nations; this information is easily spread far and wide. The nuclear genie has long been out of the bottle. Who can put it back in, when each nation fears for its very survival? The UN has been almost powerless to stop nuclear proliferation. It is therefore only a matter of time until another Hitler, Stalin, or Saddam Hussein emerges to threaten the world with nuclear weapons or some other WMD. And probably nothing short of a reign of global justice based on enforceable global law could prevent terrorists from attacking on a more massive scale than they did on September 11, 2001. Global government may also be the only way to stop the dire threat of global warming—a problem all humans share equally. Multinational treaties and UN Security Council resolutions lack the force of law and simply cannot carry out these massive tasks.

With enlightened progressives all over the world in the lead, we must move beyond the obsolete concept of a community of nations and embrace the vision of the sovereignty of the entire world's people, or face a dismal future.

True sovereignty is personal *and* global

The "one-world guerilla theatre" of world government pioneer Garry Davis dramatized that there are ultimately only two permanent and functional levels of sovereignty: the free will of the individual person—the "citizen of the world"—and the collective sovereignty of humankind as a whole. Throughout this book, we will explore the proposition that these two forms of sovereignty are irreducible, each providing a kind of bookend on one side or the other of the concept of sovereignty.

We saw earlier that leaders in Davis' generation pointed to the truth that only world government teamed with a global bill of individual rights could protect humanity in the nuclear age. But this achievement of the history of consciousness—so evident to the clearest thinkers after

WWII—was lost with the adoption of the UN charter and in the hard realities of the Cold War that descended upon the world in the early 1950s.

Courageous postwar progressives of the 1940s loudly proclaimed these great dual truths that the peoples of the world are the true sovereigns of this planet—not nation-states—and that each individual has universal rights. They produced the *Universal Declaration of Human Rights* in 1948 as a first edition of a proclamation of these principles. However, their leaders betrayed them, bequeathing to us the UN, an institution that was unable to prevent the devastating Cold War arms race—and the dozens of wars that have disgraced and disfigured our planet since that time.

Nations retain their identity in a world federation

Sovereignty transcends, but it also includes; the evolution of sovereignty does not in the least obliterate the previous levels of sovereign power. The replacement of the UN with a world government does not mean the abolition of local, national, and regional governments—it entails the *federation* of intact national (or regional) governments into a global sovereign power. Initially, nations will transfer only their war-making powers to the central government, just as the thirteen American colonies surrendered their war-making authority to the federal government, while still retaining their state militias.

It should be clear from our account that intervening "sets" of human groupings will and must exist between the level of the individual person and the "superset" called world federation. As conservative thinkers going back to Edmund Burke have shown, a political order must take measures to preserve the integrity and healthy functioning of each level of the "scaffolding" of society that exists between the individual citizen and the state—in our case, between the two fundamental levels of the *person* and the *planetary state.* This mandate includes respecting the needs and rights of such relatively sovereign units as the *family, clan, tribe, province,* and *nation*— recognizing that these evolve over time, even as the individual citizen and the planet-as-a-whole remain limits of the concept. (One can include such groupings as ethnicities, churches, political parties, labor unions, and professional associations in this list as well.)

But these transitional political and social entities are always temporary, always only of relative value in the evolution of sovereignty. What we are saying here is that vast empires, leagues of nations like the UN, nation-states, tribes, clans, and recent global contrivances such as the WTO and IMF—all organizations of power short of *personhood* and *planethood* are useful, but only insofar as they enhance the welfare and progress of the individual or of humankind as a whole.

Stated again, in the evolution of sovereignty, what are of ultimate value are the *permanently* enduring entities: the individual and the whole species. It was long ago pointed out by the philosopher John Stuart Mill that the purpose of political evolution is to foster the greatest good for the greatest number of *all* persons and for the greatest length of time. To the extent that the benefits of law and government are extended to larger and larger bodies of men and women in this way—just to that extent is there progress. If the scaffolding of any intervening and transitory level of sovereignty prevents this forward progress, then the people of the world have the sovereign right to discard or reform it. Just as Thomas Jefferson asserted that the people have the right of revolution against tyranny, so also must a *global right of rebellion* become a new rallying call for progressives longing for a peaceful and just world. As with the Founding Fathers of the United States, today's enlightened progressives will inevitably turn to the federal idea to replace our obsolete United Nations confederation.

But none of this requires that nationhood as such will be destroyed; it only means that the "absolute sovereignty" of nationhood is discarded, as real nations (and all other human groupings) become integrated into a more just and lawful political order at the global level.

Sovereignty is legitimate political power—in action

Seen in another light, sovereignty is nothing but political power. It grows by organization (and almost always by military might), and it is maintained and validated by the quality of the justice dispensed to individual persons through law and government.

By our stated criteria, the progressive growth of the organization of political power is good and proper, for it tends to encompass ever-widening segments of the total of humankind, thereby lessening the possibility of war.

But our cursory study of world history also shows that this same growth of organization creates a problem at every intervening stage. Political organizations, be they tribes, cities, or nations, are usually reluctant to trade a portion of their sovereignty to gain the benefits of an expanded rule of law. People instinctively fear rule by "foreigners" whenever any federation of powers is contemplated. But as history shows, the benefits accruing from the extension of the rule of law outweigh the risk of tyranny at all levels of government.

By the same token, many people rightly fear global

government because of the downside possibility that vicious minorities might gain control. It is possible, of course, for any government to become tyrannical. A good constitution that guarantees rights and a separation of powers does not carry a guarantee that courts will uphold the laws or that the executive branch will enforce them. The constitution of the Soviet Union was in many ways a progressive document, but was generally ignored; the policies that Hitler pursued were considered legal under German law as it evolved under Nazism; in the US, Congresspersons of both parties voted the Bush administration's Patriot Act into law. What do these dangers point to? In the end, the burden of freedom always falls on the true sovereigns, not on government bureaucrats and politicians who are always subject to the temptations of corruption; it is the citizens' responsibility to make sure that government serves the needs of the people and is true to the democratic intent of its creators.

Yes, a global government could become tyrannical, but then *any* government or organization can become corrupt. Shall we therefore eliminate all government or all organizations? Shall we fail to institute government where it is needed, narrowing our vision to the status quo? Shall we say that it makes sense to have local, state, and national governments, but that it would be wrong and dangerous to have a global government? What is it about the global level of government that changes this equation? These questions will be addressed as we go.

But one fact is obvious: Presently, if a foreign country attacks another country, the latter has no choice but to fight back, either alone or through a treaty alliance. When Japan attacked Pearl Harbor, the US had no choice but to defend itself by declaring war and creating a giant war machine. If one country is determined to violate the supposed sovereign rights of another, the only way to stop the aggression is to go to war—risking the use of WMDs or even world war. Under a global government, such foreign invasions will be outlawed; all military forces come under the control of the world body insofar as they cross national borders, and global law, democratically agreed upon and enforced by global marshals and a world police force, governs the actions of individual nations in global affairs.

In truth, living under a system of war and anarchy with WMDs readily available for use on the field of battle—*that* is the really frightening choice when it is compared with tyranny. Under a constitutional system of global government, political crimes will surely be committed, but they will be dealt with by the world police force and court system; a democratic world legislature will represent the eyes and ears of the world's people; political parties at the global level will compete for power on the basis of the fruits of peace and prosperity that they offer. One wonders how this can be seen as inferior to relying on a war system that allows nation-states the unlimited sovereign power to attack one another at will and permits corporations to plunder the global environment outside the rule of law.

There are great challenges at each step between the two enduring levels of the individual person and the final consummation of political growth—i.e., the federal government of all humankind, by all humankind, and for all humankind.

At the moment, our world is stalled in a quagmire of nationhood, held up by centuries of inertia from proceeding toward planethood. The problem facing us at this stage is the *delusion* of national sovereignty, especially when linked to the corrupting influences of war profiteering, religious fundamentalism, and rapacious global banks and corporations.

The hard truth is this: The concept of the absolute sovereignty of the nation-state is the profound political problem of our time—it is a transitory form that has served its purpose. Nation-states were first created to ensure basic law and order within their boundaries, but today they can no longer claim to provide even the most basic protections. When we wake up each day with the fear that a repeat performance of a terrorist attack like that of 9/11 is imminent, then we need to realize that it is time to move to the next level of sovereignty.

Our forebears in the late 1940s knew that the nuclear age had brought about a sea change. The proliferation of weapons of mass destruction in a world of international anarchy has created an unprecedented set of dangers. The nation-state as a provider of security and protection is bankrupt. *There is no state in the world that can now provide reliable security.* When the state can no longer fulfill its basic purpose, then it is time for reform. Progressives should be the first to realize that people have a right of rebellion against the spurious notion of the absolute sovereignty of the nation-state. The people of the nations of the world must transfer their war-making powers to a world federation, based on the dual recognition of the sovereignty of all humankind and the intrinsic rights of all individuals—or face catastrophe. The global governance movement is not trying to build a utopia; rather, it is urgently trying to prevent worldwide disaster.

> *A federation of all humanity . . . would mean*
> *such a release and increase of human energy as*
> *to open up a new phase in human history.*
> —H.G. Wells

2

The Case for
Global Law

World federalism is an idea that will not die.
More and more people are coming to realize that peace
must be more than an interlude if we are to survive;
that peace is a product of law and order; that law is
essential if the force of arms is not to rule the world.

—William O. Douglas
Former US Supreme Court Justice

Today's enlightened progressives have an unprecedented opportunity. As advocates of democracy—as the global democrats of the future—we are in the best position to represent the great truth that *the world's people,* and not the world's nation-states, are the true sovereigns of this planet.

But we must also be magnanimous and include another radical perspective. Imagine that we have colleagues who are global libertarians, and they have formed their own global political party that one day will sit just across the aisle from us in the world legislature. They will insist that, alongside the people's sovereignty, we must observe the equally important principle of *individual accountability* before global law. This principle, they will say, is based on the notion of the irreducible free-will sovereignty of the individual. Its corollary idea, they will probably maintain, is the central importance of creating a global constitution with a universal bill of rights that will protect the rights of individuals—including voting rights—in relation to the global sovereignty of all humankind for which we, the global democrats, are the primary advocates.

We've seen how progressives can be empowered in this futuristic work by tracing our lineage back to the "one world" generation of the 1940s. We believe it is incumbent upon today's progressives to pick up this torch once again.

Leadership entails making the essentials clear. This chapter breaks out a key feature of the discussion of chapter one by asking how enlightened progressives can take the lead in offering the world's people a choice:

The force of law versus *the law of force.*

Today's progressives already fight the excesses of the American empire, but now we must perform double duty: We argue here that progressives must also cut through the illusions of "collective security" via multinational treaties or the actions of the Security Council within the United Nations. We must tell all who will listen that it is time to choose between enforceable global law based on democratic deliberation, or the law of force in a world of anarchy. And in doing so, enlightened progressives must carry out yet another feat: To win on a global platform, they will also need to hold the space for both sides of the concept of sovereignty: the hard-won notion of the collective sovereignty of the world's people, and the equally essential truth of the rights and duties of the individual world citizen before global law.

A simple truth:
Peace requires the rule of law

It is a truism that, through slow and painful evolution, the *rule of law* has progressed steadily over the centuries. The benefits of this process can be seen everywhere today, but of course only *inside* national borders. Especially noteworthy is the peace and social harmony that results when the rule of law is extended to large national federations such as those in Canada, India, the European Union, and the United States, where citizens do not worry about their states or provinces going to war against each other. Throughout the world, most countries are relatively civilized within their own borders by virtue of the rule of their own native laws, backed up by their own homeland police and defense forces as well as some system of justice through civil and criminal courts.

As a thought experiment, consider for a moment what the US would be like if the federal government and federal law were somehow removed, and each of its fifty states were rendered an independent country with its own president, currency, and national laws. A traveler who was a New York state citizen would need a passport, for example, to go from New York to New Jersey. Businesspeople selling products across the former US territory would have to deal with fifty different currencies and fifty different versions of contract law. Each nation-state would need to have its own standing army, and some nations would surely produce and stockpile WMDs in addition to their conventional arms. Some "countries" would be more socialistic (let's say Vermont, California, Massachusetts) while others might be ultra-capitalist (perhaps Texas, Oklahoma, and Utah) and even aggressive toward other nations. One can imagine how likely it would be that small wars would break out from time to time—or even large wars, as these nation-states band together in treaty alliances for "collective security." Imagine, for example, that Colorado and Arizona were facing a serious drought and began to dispute with one another over water rights involving the use of the Colorado River for irrigation. Given the absence of federal law and courts, they would be forced to go to war to settle their dispute if negotiations did not work out. Neighboring states or "treaty allies" might find themselves joining one side or the other, jostling for advantage in the conflict. Before long the situation might degenerate into a conflagration, ending with a nuclear confrontation.

This may sound a bit absurd, but this scenario is not far from depicting the state of international relations today. Whenever and wherever the rule of force (and not the rule of law) applies, war becomes a legitimate option for settling disputes—and the preparation for wars of defense becomes a necessity.

Of course, individuals in a civilized society do not have the option of resorting to violence to settle their disputes; a monopoly on violence is reserved for the state in connection with law enforcement or due process of law. Vigilante justice, revenge killings, intrusive surveillance, undercover espionage, and in general taking the law into one's own hands are illegal for individuals, but all this and much worse is accepted as normal between nation-states—especially the strongest ones. Individuals must follow laws and limit their behavior accordingly, but nations, lacking a sovereign authority above them, may act without restraint if they can get away with it.

One can see how the option of law versus force offers such a stark choice. Lasting peace comes only from order that is based on law backed by the enforcement power of democratic government. That's why enforceable law is the antidote to anarchy. The *rule of law* at the global level is the only means by which the human race will be able to establish peace. Such an enduring peace is qualitatively different from a "truce." A truce is based on an uneasy balance of power that usually marks the interim between wars; whereas genuine peace is the presence of order and justice, produced by law, which is the product of representative government.

Hopefully, a stable peace based on global law will one day grace this world. The greatest planetary achievements in science, industry, human relations, and the arts must await those great times. The essential point is that these more advanced things are enabled by one very basic thing: peace and justice through the *rule of law.*

"Law," the poet Mark Van Doren once explained, "is merely the thing that lets us live in peace with our neighbors without having to love them." Enforceable law is not nearly as good a thing as spiritual consciousness or moral maturity, and it is certainly no substitute for personal spiritual growth. But without basic guarantees of security, humans can regress to the animal aggression that is in the biological heritage of our species. In a state of anarchy and war, we tend to forget about love and tolerance.

History provides proof that the rule of law is indispensable for avoiding the spiral of violence and mistrust that anarchy always creates. Law is in fact the prerequisite for generating sufficient amounts of good will in daily life so that a society based on love, tolerance, and compassion may have a chance to evolve—as these things cannot be directly legislated. Love and law always seem to arise together in this symbiotic fashion.

Thus it cannot be said enough: The only way to abolish war entirely is to establish the just rule of enforceable world law. If we can find the political will to achieve this great victory, the resulting reign of peace will in time produce the mutual trust and security between peoples and nations that could create a worldwide cultural and spiritual renaissance. This in turn would lay the basis for almost unimaginable levels of material and spiritual prosperity on a worldwide scale.

Legislators can quickly adapt global laws to global needs

The rule of law provides peace and stability, but it is also *dynamic*. The great advantage of representative government is that it permits orderly change and adaptation through deliberative assemblies of legislators, whereas a confederation of nations like the United Nations tends to be a *guardian of the status quo*. Without legislation and the ongoing interpretation of new laws by courts, law cannot and will not evolve. Without ever-improving applications of law as determined by democratic forums in touch with everyday needs of all sectors of society, social relations soon stagnate.

Meanwhile, social conditions continue along their own trajectory. Largely oblivious to the operations of government, *life conditions* continue to undergo epochal changes because of technological change or shifts in population. The result is in an ever-increasing lag between the functions of government and the realities on the ground.

This may explain why today's international relations are in an advanced level of stagnation bordering on decadence. The UN reflected the needs of the world just after WWII, but it has not changed substantively since. The sad fact about the UN, according to Tad Daley, who led the Campaign for a New UN Charter, is that the UN was maladapted even for the post-WWII era:

> Most of the architecture of the United Nations system was created at the end of World War II in a dramatically different international environment [from today]. Much of their design was directed at addressing the political and economic dislocations of the immediate postwar world. Indeed, the

collective security mechanism at the heart of the UN Charter was arguably directed not even at the world of 1945, but the world of the 1930s. By far the central issue on the minds of the framers who met in San Francisco in April, May, and June of 1945 was "How do we prevent another Adolf Hitler?" But long-term issues like global environmental degradation are infinitely different from a Panzer blitzkrieg across the Polish border. We want to consider what kinds of global governance structures might be appropriate not for the world of the 1930s, but for the world of the twenty-first century.[1]

It is tragic indeed that today's politicians have not responded to the imperative of adapting our international institutions to evolving global realities; but we believe a new generation of progressives can and will do what needs to be done.

We must distinguish between the causes and effects of anarchy

The tried and true solution to anarchy is just one thing: law and government. In all places and throughout history, government's chief task in civil society is to first establish enforceable rules for resolving conflicts between individuals and groups without violence.

Why do cities or states within a nation no longer engage in warfare with each other? The answer has to do with *relinquishing sovereignty.*

As we have seen, war between groups of people organized into social units—tribes, cities, or nations—takes place when these groups exercise unrestricted sovereign power. When there is no higher authority to resolve conflicts on the basis of law and judicial processes, then chaos and war are the only options. War ceases the moment sovereign power is transferred to a larger or higher unit. War takes place when separate groups of equal sovereignty come into conflict. When sovereignty was transferred to the nation, wars between cities and tribes ceased.

Peace is possible only when a new sovereign source of law is set up over and above the old clashing groups, creating an integrated whole and a higher source of law. Pollution across national boundaries will cease when enforceable global laws are passed to prevent it.

Armed with this understanding, we can stop confusing *causes* and effects and start treating the cause of war and in justice—not just the symptoms. The chief cause of war and terrorism is unlimited national sovereignty and the absence of global law—*not* the weapons these perpetrators might happen to use.

It is a positive step when citizens protest a particular war or rally for nuclear disarmament. But this type of action addresses only the symptoms of a war system based on unlimited national sovereignty. Today we must do away with the entire war system, not just with the weapons of war or any particular war.

In the final analysis, people resort to violence not because their race or nationality are prone to violence, not because they intrinsically lack love and decency in their hearts, not because they possess particular weapons, but *because they are hopelessly frustrated* by the fact that they have no legislative or judicial forum in which their grievances can be heard and adjudicated.

The cause of global warming is not simply carbon emissions and thoughtless, wanton drivers of sport utility vehicles; it is the lack of an enforceable global agreement to actually reduce these emissions. Rapacious corporations are not the cause of child labor in Indonesia; these corporations are able to run amuck in the developing world because of the lack of enforceable global laws that would outlaw child labor. The cause of sweatshop labor in Mexico is not simply the greed of some corporate CEO—we will always have greed in commerce—but the lack of a global legislature that represents the interests of all people, including working people.

Legally speaking, the perpetrators of violent international conflict are the *individuals* issuing orders to attack and kill, not entire nations. Perpetrators of global pollution or labor exploitation are specific, identifiable individuals. We need to transform the peace and environmental movements into a powerful force for the creation of a cure for the true causes of war, pollution, and poverty—a global democratic government based on world law that applies to real individuals. Law creates individual accountability—the very basis of a just society. The lack of individual accountability under enforceable law is the true cause of the global problems we face.

"International law" is a misnomer

Currently, nations have little binding power to control irresponsible behavior by other states—i.e., those individual heads of states who may engage in evils such as aggression, pollution, or nuclear proliferation. Today's so-called system of international law, the foundation of our current system of treaties, is a sad and appalling misnomer.

Too long has our world witnessed the tragic results of the current system of treaties based on international law. No matter how significant a given treaty may seem, all such international agreements are flawed in that they permit all the prerogatives of sovereignty to remain with the agreeing parties.

It cannot be said enough: International "law" is a myth.

Under its supposed reign, parties are free to ignore with impunity the treaty obligations that are the basis of international law. They can do this because there is no global government with the power to hold these states accountable. But law is not truly law unless it is enforceable. Law proclaims that there is something that one must or must not do, with the understanding that failure to comply will result in specific consequences to the lawbreaker that are meted out by a legitimate government. Law requires the existence of government to enforce it; law will never exist without government until those far-distant utopian times when men and women are entirely self-governing.

Treaties have, in a sense, been helpful in laying the foundation for world law, but as any Native American knows, treaties do not protect the weaker party from the likelihood that the stronger side will not honor its end of the bargain when it sees an advantage. Since there is no third party to enforce the treaty, any party to a treaty can fail to live up to its promise with impunity. The Bush administration's decision to pull out of the Anti-Ballistic Missile (ABM) Treaty in order to proceed with its National Missile Defense System, and North Korea's withdrawal from the Nuclear Non-Proliferation Treaty, exemplify this problem. International law has evolved over the last century and in many ways has become more effective, but until the world forms a third-party enforcement mechanism, and until global government replaces the current system of treaties, international law will continue to be unenforceable and ultimately ineffective.

A global system based on treaties is also weakened by the fact that only those nations who have ratified a treaty are obliged to abide by it. When a nation chooses not to sign a given treaty, or to unilaterally withdraw from a treaty, as many do, it obviously has no obligation to follow that particular agreement. When a system of world law replaces international law, a world legislature will pass laws that apply uniformly to the whole world—or at least to those countries that are members of the federation.

It is futile to try to establish world peace via the threat of nuclear terror, or by treaties, alliances, or an unstable balance of power between the largest states. If we are to create something that has never existed—enduring world peace and justice—we must be willing to build something that has never existed: democratic global government.

Global law is meaningful only if it is enforceable

We are living today under a flawed international system with nearly two hundred nations that are each virtually a law unto themselves. However, business and commerce must be conducted. The channels of trade and travel must be safeguarded—somehow. Something must fill the vacuum that is created by the absence of a world government to enforce global law to keep the peace. And given the failure of the United Nations, that role will, by default, fall to the world's largest military and economic powers and to an unenforceable, unreliable body of international treaties.

As progressives well know, in the last decade the US has rushed into the power vacuum caused by the end of the Cold War and the abiding weaknesses of the UN system. We are now faced with the prospect of unchecked military domination of our planet by its sole remaining superpower. And this self-assumed American hegemonic role has great importance in the evolution of global law. It is perversely teaching us about one feature of the coming world government to which we have already alluded: In the absence of world law, firm enforcement of some other sort of international order is still needed in a dangerous world in which lanes of commerce must be kept open. In the absence of a democratic world government, a "new world order" will be provided by default by the world's largest superpower.

In recent times, all US administrations, both Democratic and Republican, have dressed up their overseas interventions with a rhetoric that attributes their motives to the enforcement of the broader interests of the civilized world. One can clearly see the accent on "enforcement." For example, in his ultimatum speech to Saddam Hussein just before the US invasion of Iraq in March 2003, George W. Bush's speechwriters dubbed our intervention as "enforcement of the just demands of the world." Sadly, the Bush administration co-opted the language of global justice even as it perpetrated a unilateral, preemptive intervention on a sovereign nation. Rather than seize the dictator himself and apply some feature of existing international law against this one individual in a world court, the Americans were forced for the second time in slightly more than a decade to lead a war against an entire people. And this came after many years of US-led UN sanctions against Iraq that decimated their economy while leaving a brutal dictator in power— precisely the opposite result of what could have been achieved by applying the principle of individual accountability!

Truly, our options remain stark: To restate, the essential choice is between the force of global law applied against individuals in a governed world, or the law of force applied against whole countries in a world dominated by nation-states and a military superpower. America must decide whether it will be an obstacle to world law or a leader in the development of global democratic institutions. It is as simple as that.

A complicated world like ours needs decisive enforcement of legitimate global law against individual lawbreakers, such as terrorists, drug traffickers, and dictators. But without it, high-minded phrases such as "the just demands of the world" and "international law" will become linguistic fodder for the reigning superpower. Propagandists in the US State Department (or leaders of any other superpower) will use such language to justify their own nationalistic and self-serving enforcement of illegitimate "laws" against entire countries. In the absence of a global institution representing the world's people, which is empowered to enforce just laws of our own making, the US—or institutions it dominates such as the WTO, IMF, and World Bank—will always be happy to step in with its own interpretation of what is needed to keep the peace. In the new model that we propose in this book, law enforcement will instead be embedded in the context of a genuine global democracy—a global governing structure that represents the will and reflects the sovereignty of the world's people.

Global law requires global courts of justice

Among the first planks of any global constitution will be the abolition of war between nations and the binding adjudication of international disputes and criminal acts by legitimate world courts. The first imperative of world civilization is to outlaw murder of all kinds across national boundaries, and to use legitimate force to hold individual lawbreakers—and not entire nations like Iraq or Afghanistan—accountable before legitimate standards of world justice. And as the world government applies global law against individuals, world courts will develop case law that interprets the global constitution and enhances our understanding of the human rights that will no doubt be enshrined in a global bill of rights. We as individuals must follow laws and limit our behavior accordingly. In a civilized and governed world, nations too must follow laws that limit and control their behavior.

Oddly enough, back in early 2003, just as the Bush administration was descending into its role as arbiter and sole enforcer of a spurious "global law" of its own making, the true alternative to this scenario was quietly emerging and was briefly noted on the back pages of newspapers. The attack on Iraq was perhaps one of the worst events in international relations; but what was arguably the best moment in global diplomatic history occurred in the very same month—the seating of the eighteen justices at the International Criminal Court (ICC) in The Hague. This positive development was the mirror opposite of what Bush was foisting on the world.

The timing was remarkable. Although opposed at all points by the Bush administration, the ICC, as of March 11, 2003 was officially inaugurated in The Hague, where eleven men and seven women—selected from a list of the world's finest jurists—were honored at a gala presided over by Queen Beatrix of the Netherlands. The inaugural ceremony was attended by foreign ministers and international diplomats from one hundred countries—and of course was totally absent of representatives from the United States.

We cite this example because the ICC is the progenitor of the coming system of genuine world courts. However, the coming world legislature, based on individual suffrage, has no precedent at the global level and will have to be created from scratch. Progressives who have achieved a global level of political consciousness should be in the forefront of this historic undertaking, which we discuss in more detail in the coming chapters.

Enforceable world law is
an idea whose time has come

Enforceable global law will not be achieved by revolution; it will be an evolutionary accomplishment of humankind.

We envision a gradual process that will be punctuated by a few sudden breakthroughs. For example, the breakthrough to the creation of the ICC—however flawed—put in place one more building block of progress. When the Security Council stood up for the UN Charter by confronting the US over its plan to invade Iraq, this too was a positive step in the direction of enforceable global law. Perhaps a provisional world legislature will evolve that could pass advisory laws that would approximate an expression of the sovereignty of the world's people. The accumulation of many small victories of this sort will eventually lead to a transformation in global governance.

At the moment, however, the momentum of forward progress is too slow. Global civilization is in an accelerating state of change, but the evolution of international law is stagnant—frozen like a deer in the headlights of progress. Nuclear weapons and WMDs have spread everywhere, the environment is collapsing, and economic globalization is rapidly overtaking the planet, but our political institutions and especially the United Nations are far behind in their adaptation.

Conditions are ripe for change. The great goal of the abolition of war stands just before us, representing the pinnacle of the advancement of civilization through the force of law. Outlawing war will allow a vast shift of resources from the war system to the betterment of the human condition. This precedent will lead to global environmental protection and other just laws. The *Pax Romana* of the Roman empire and the peace now enjoyed within the United States illustrate advantages of coming together to form a union. When war is replaced by law, greatness becomes possible.

We are a link in the human chain of evolution. We owe a debt to those who came before us, some of whom gave their lives for the blessings we now enjoy. We need to be a strong link in the chain between this legacy and the immediate future. It is our opportunity to be either a generation of glory or a generation of shame. Let it not be said that we were the link that broke. Let it instead be celebrated that we were the generation that found the courage to face this truth: Enforceable global law is the answer to global problems. As Harris Wofford, the founder in the 1940s of the Student Federalists, once said, we are engaged in "the revolution to establish politically the brotherhood of man."

Our ideal is a world community of states which
are based on the rule of law and which subordinate
their foreign policy activities to law.
—Mikhail Gorbachev

3

From World Citizenship to World Democracy

I am a citizen, not of Athens or Greece, but of the world.
—Socrates

By virtue of physically inhabiting the same planet, human beings everywhere suffer in common from such maladies as nuclear proliferation, global warming, and the war system that forces every country to waste vast resources on arms. We live in a world in which oppressed groups lack legal recourse for their grievances in global courts; as a result, people everywhere are faced with the possibility of being caught up in a terrorist event or a war perpetrated by such oppressed groups. The horrors of 9/11 were not just limited to the US; images of these attacks sent emotional shockwaves to people in all countries, and terrorists soon thereafter mounted devastating attacks from Bali to Spain. In the wake of these tragedies, governments everywhere have had to institute unprecedented repressive measures in order to engage in the so-called "war on terrorism." In addition, virtually everyone now shares in the vicissitudes of the global economy. International financial speculation has, for example, often caused grievous effects in unpredictable places—such as the collapse of the Mexican peso in 1995 and the so-called Asia meltdown in 1997. We have just begun to see how vulnerable all of us are in the face of our economic interdependence.

This is the short list of shared global problems in which everyone has a stake; nearly every literate adult in the world holds opinions on such matters that, by all rights, should be accounted for in a democratic global forum.

Obviously, there is no such forum. Whether you are Mexican or Mongolian or American, you really have no direct say, *as an individual,* in such global matters. Your voice is mute. And your vote is not wanted.

The sad fact is, in today's global anarchy, each and every individual suffers from systematic legal and political disenfranchisement at the global level. Our individual vote is *never* acknowledged as a factor in determining how humankind is to cope with its common problems. Powerful nations like America may have more global access to political power than other nations, but certainly not Americans as *individuals.* What can be done about this?

We need political enfranchisement at the global level

We saw in the last chapter that in the absence of global law, our right to "life, liberty, and the pursuit of happiness" has no legal status at the global level. Our national governments may and do speak for us on global matters, but this representation usually occurs in forums such as the United Nations, which only recognize national sovereignty, or in institutions such as the WTO and IMF that have no democratic accountability.

Let's try a thought experiment to illustrate our current disenfranchisement dilemma. Imagine the effects in your personal life if the federal government, the US Constitution, and the Bill of Rights were somehow eliminated in a civil war and the United States was turned into a miniaturized version of today's United Nations—a "United Nations" of fifty confederated states. Let's say that, like the real UN, the American confederation had organized itself around a General Assembly and a Security Council that consisted of the five biggest states: Texas, New York, California, Florida, and Pennsylvania, and that the seat of the confederation were Dallas, Texas.

Now, just like the UN system, there would be no right to vote for representatives to this confederation government; these would be appointed by the state governments as *ambassadors* to the General Assembly.

Within any one of the fifty nations, there may or may not be a bill of rights. In some earlier civil disturbances, many nations, such as Texas, had been taken over by dictators. A few of the nations, such as Vermont, were controlled by parties from the far left.

Let's run an example of "international terrorism" through this model. Imagine that your house in Michigan, near the Ohio border, was destroyed in a sudden attack by a group of Ohioans. The terrorists from Ohio then rushed back across the border before the Michigan military was able to apprehend them. To get any redress in the matter, you would have to appeal to the seat of government in Michigan, in hopes that they would have a treaty with Ohio that would allow Michigan authorities to deal with the violence across its borders. Even if there were such a treaty, you would have to get Michigan's ambassador to Ohio to convince the government of Ohio to act in the matter, according to its own domestic laws that may apply to treaty enforcement. Ohio would have the sole discretion as to whether or not it should act on treaty enforcement against its renegade terrorists. If that effort were unsuccessful, Michigan could not act directly against these aggressors. It would have to seek a resolution from the Security Council in Dallas, Texas, calling for sanctions against *the entire state of Ohio*—or even to go to war against Ohio!

You have now learned some hard lessons: 1) within the territory of the confederation, you have no individual legal rights; 2) the Ohio terrorists have no legal accountability outside of Ohio; 3) there is no court in which you can take legal action as an individual; and 4) you have no vote in the matter, because there are no elections of direct representatives to the confederation government.

If you were very wealthy, you might act through the ambassador from Michigan seeking to get the Dallas government to somehow influence the Security Council to act on this matter—only to have it vetoed by the ambassador from Ohio!

This absurd example illustrates how on the world stage—given the United Nations system as it is today—each human subsists *without legal and political rights*. We say this notwithstanding the existence of human rights covenants such as the Universal Declaration of Human Rights, and the ICC (International Criminal Court) treaty.

Individual accountability at the global level is an imperative

We manifestly lack global protection of our legal and political rights. But neither do we as individuals have binding *obligations* or responsibilities to the world community.

International law, such as it is, lays down norms for behavior based on international treaties. But in these documents, individuals are classified as *citizens of nation-states,* and *not* as global citizens who are accountable to a global government. Actual enforcement of these treaties against individuals only occurs within the country of citizenship, if at all. That country must have passed specific legislation requiring enforcement of a given treaty on its citizens. And it must also be willing to actually use these domestic laws to enforce the treaty provisions against them, applying penalties measured out according to domestic law, *not* international law.

Another of the many flaws of this system is that a given treaty may or may not have been agreed upon by the nation in which a violator has citizenship. For example, as of 2004, major polluters in the US were technically not subject to obligations under international law concerning the environment. This is because the US government withdrew from the Kyoto Accords on Climate Control and is also not party to the Convention on Biological Diversity.

The Geneva Convention Relative to the Treatment of Prisoners of War has long been universally agreed upon by treaty, but events in Iraq have demonstrated that even this prestigious covenant has little binding power if a nation-state has another agenda. There has been no legal recourse for the individual Iraqis who were tortured or killed when the US military perpetrated egregious violations of the provisions of the Geneva Conventions at the Abu Ghraib prison in Iraq in 2003 and 2004. Mild disciplinary actions were brought by Pentagon authorities against the immediate perpetrators, but the international outcry for greater accountability for these crimes stopped there. Secretary of Defense Donald Rumsfeld opposed strict observance of the Geneva Conventions in Iraq, and he literally waived the application of the Geneva Conventions to the war in Afghanistan and for the "prisoner of war" camp at Guantanamo Bay, Cuba. Responsibility for this policy was traced all the way up to President Bush, but there has been no individual accountability for these acts before the world or the Iraqi people through the agencies of international law.

As we noted in the last chapter, we are now witnessing an encouraging breakthrough (outside of the US) with respect to individual accountability for the most egregious criminal acts. Criminal statutes at the global level that will actually apply to individuals are now evolving through the launch of the first prosecutions by the International Criminal Court.

Ad hoc tribunals and the ICC mark a beginning

It all began with the Tokyo Trials and especially the Nuremberg Trials at the end of WWII, which later resulted in the adoption of the Nuremberg Principles in 1950 by the UN. In general, the Nuremberg Principles extend the jurisdiction of international law to criminal acts, clearly stating that individuals—including heads of state—are to be held responsible for criminal behavior in international settings even if their own domestic law does not hold them accountable, and are entitled to a fair trial in an international court. The Principles listed three types of crimes under international law: crimes against peace, war crimes, and crimes against humanity.

Perhaps the best-known of the seven Nuremberg Principles is Principle IV, which resulted from the trial defense strategy used by Nazi underlings in which they claimed that they were "only following orders." The principle states that following orders "does not relieve [a defendant] from responsibility under international law, provided a moral choice was in fact possible to him."

Though obviously unenforceable, these Principles have been used as an important reference for governments and military organizations ever since they were promulgated. More important, the UN Security Council has used Nuremberg as a precedent for prosecuting egregious war crimes through ad hoc tribunals that the UN has created by fiat. Though expensive and cumbersome, and usually too late to stop the perpetration itself, these tribunals have been a step in the right direction toward holding the worst international criminals accountable.

The most important of these has been the International Criminal Tribunal for the Former Yugoslavia. This ad hoc tribunal was established by a UN Security Council resolution in the face of the serious violations of international humanitarian law by Serbian President Slobodan Milosevic and other collaborators. In May 1999, when Milosevic was indicted by this tribunal, he became the first head of state ever to be indicted by an international court. It is precedents like these that the new world government will build upon as it puts in place clear principles for individual accountability under global law.

However, more often in the·decades since WWII, the UN has not met the challenge of creating such tribunals. It has instead followed the procedure of applying sanctions that, in effect, hold entire populations of countries accountable for the perpetration of international crimes by their leaders. Perhaps the worst case of this fundamentally immoral procedure of collective punishment under international law is that of Iraq. The whole world knows that the Iraqis have paid immeasurably for the behavior of one man, Saddam Hussein, through two wars and the UN's devastating economic sanctions during the intervening period between these costly wars.

The movement for the ICC—which now establishes a permanent tribunal—arose in part because of the moral outrage over the failure of sanctions against Iraq, and the widely noted "collateral damage" these had caused to the people of Iraq. Another motivating factor was the genocide in Rwanda—perhaps the greatest single example of the UN's inability to stop war crimes. The UN has also created an International Criminal Tribunal for Rwanda, many years after the atrocities were committed.

The ICC's charter builds directly upon the Nuremberg Principles and other established norms of international law. The visionary jurists behind the Nuremberg Principles long ago called for a permanent criminal court; the ICC is much of their dream become reality.

As of its formal establishment in March 2003, the ICC is now an independent criminal court and is not considered part of the United Nations system. It is a standing, permanent body, located in The Hague (Netherlands) just adjacent to the World Court, formally known as the International Court of Justice. The World Court is a civil court concerned solely with legal disputes between nations. The ICC's sole purpose is to investigate and bring to justice *individuals* who commit genocide, crimes against humanity, and war crimes—but only when a nation in which a perpetrator resides is unwilling or unable to do so. Importantly, because most wars in the last fifty years have been civil wars, the ICC has jurisdiction over crimes committed during both international and internal conflicts.

The signatories to the ICC are known as State Parties. A crime prosecuted by the ICC must meet one of four criteria: It must have been committed in the territory of a State Party; by a citizen of a State Party; when a non-member accepts the Court's jurisdiction; or when the UN Security Council refers a case to the ICC, regardless of whether the countries involved are State Parties.

The ICC arose out of the so-called Rome Statute, and the organizing movement that led to the adoption of the Rome Statute in 1998 was carried out by a large number of NGOs (non-governmental organizations) led by the World Federalist Movement, and in particular by its executive director Bill Pace. The ICC Treaty that resulted from the Rome Statute has now been ratified by ninety-four nations. Terrorism, crimes of aggression, and drug trafficking are presently excluded from the statute, at least until the ICC's seven-year review conference in 2009.

The Rome Statute includes extensive due process provisions. These include all the rights of the accused that are guaranteed by the International Covenant on Civil and Political Rights. These include the presumption of innocence, the right to counsel, the right to confront one's accusers, the right to a speedy trial, protection against double jeopardy, and prohibition of trial in absentia. In fact, defendants at the ICC are guaranteed all of the same due process provisions as are present in US courts, with the single exception of trial by jury.

The ICC cannot impose a death penalty; those found guilty will be held in a prison in The Hague. The court can also order convicted criminals to pay reparations to the people and communities they harmed. Victims can participate in sentencing and sentence reduction hearings.

In the recent past, the inevitable delay in the creation of ad hoc tribunals sometimes resulted in the destruction of evidence while perpetrators remained at large. The ICC, however, will be able to respond to crimes as they occur, and it is believed that its permanence will deter future criminals. It is also hoped that the ICC's influence will prompt national courts to hold their own citizens accountable.

The ICC is a real advance for humanity, for the universal recognition of human rights, and for the principle of individual accountability. However, its problems are obvious and its loopholes are many. First of all, the ICC does not have an independent police force. It must rely on countries to extradite suspects to The Hague. More important is the fact that the ICC is "extra-constitutional." Its powers are not limited by a world constitution that is based on the democratic sovereignty of the world's people. A world constitution would naturally put in place a global bill of rights, and defend these rights with the force of law applied to individuals. It would also guarantee protection against abuse through a constitutional separation of powers.

World citizenship is no longer a mere sentiment

The ICC has opened the door to individual accountability before world law for the worst international criminals, but our real goal is a movement for a democratic world federation that would bring about the legal and political enfranchisement *and* accountability of each of the six billion individuals on earth.

It is only through a global bill of rights, along with world courts and police to enforce and interpret these rights, and through the right to elect delegates to a world legislature, that we truly become *citizens of the world*. Our world citizenship is then no longer a mere sentiment, no longer a hollow pronouncement of idealistic philosophers; its rights and obligations are consecrated in a world constitution that applies to all humans equally, and for all time.

The Nuremberg Principles were the beginning of the end of a world beset by fear and alienation, and they accomplished this by establishing the principle of individual conscience as a category of international law. The grand transition to world government will mark the end of our political alienation from one another as fellow humans. It is one crucial step in the materialization of the brotherhood and sisterhood of all human beings that many world religions have proclaimed. When this transition finally occurs, it will be based on the intrinsic, inalienable political and spiritual free will of individuals, and all the rights and obligations that flow from that.

Global activism for world citizenship is needed now

As a philosopher might put it, each person is inherently self-sovereign. But our inherent rights as sovereign individuals are trampled upon by the current system of sovereign nation-states. How can we go about securing our rights and obligations under world law?

It requires nothing less than global activism, a subject we will glance at here but return to in Part III of this book.

In the first chapter we examined the dramatic scene in 1948 when WWII veteran Garry Davis—the first great activist for world citizenship—interrupted a session of the United Nations General Assembly to speak rhetorically on behalf of the world's people. World citizenship as a concept has been discussed and theorized from the days of Socrates, but it required an event like WWII to bring about the public launch of the movement for world citizenship. These were the words Davis delivered in November 1948 to the General Assembly as it convened at the Palais de Chaillot in Paris:

Mister Chairman and delegates!

I interrupt you in the name of the people of the world not represented here. Though my words may be unheeded,

> our common need for world law and order can no longer be
> disregarded.
>
> We, the people, want the peace which only a world
> government can give. The sovereign states you represent
> divide us and lead us to the abyss of Total War. I call upon
> you to no longer deceive us by this illusion of political author-
> ity. I call upon you to convene forthwith a World Constituent
> Assembly to raise the standard round which all men can
> gather, the standard of true peace, of One Government for
> One World.
>
> And if you fail us in this . . . stand aside. For a People's
> World Assembly will arise from our own ranks to create such
> a government. We can be served by nothing less.[1]

Worldwide support for this speech, which came to be called the Oran Declaration, included prominent thinkers such as Albert Einstein, Albert Camus, Albert Schweitzer, and Richard Wright.

Davis's next step was to found the International Registry of World Citizens. Within a few years, over 750,000 individuals in 150 countries registered.

Davis did not stop there. On September 4, 1953, from the Town Hall of Ellsworth, Maine, he declared the founding of what he called the World Government of World Citizens based on the simple assertion of our inherent legal rights as human beings.[2]

Davis's work is a precedent for the global activists of the future who will enshrine world citizenship as a cornerstone of a democratic global government.

We live in an increasingly interconnected, interdependent, and globalized world. Just about everything we encounter in everyday life has become subject to globalization, including business, agriculture, commerce, entertainment, media, science, medicine, and the environment—that is, everything except democracy and social justice. The world has globalized, but our global political institutions are relics of the past.

Democracy is perhaps the only instrument of civilization that continues to be confined within local and national boundaries. For the same reason, enforceable law that protects the rights of individuals remains confined within the arbitrary limits of the place of nationality. We are born as individual humans on this unique and wonderful planet, but we are branded by birth certificates as Russian, American, or Chinese. It is time to claim our true identities as world citizens in order to gain the rights and privileges that global government can offer.

The way out of this predicament is for the people of the world to rise up and assume control of their destiny through a forum that directly reflects their collective sovereignty. This forum will be the coming world legislature. The constitution, bill of rights, and laws that are acted upon by this legislature will protect the sacredness of our individual rights.

> *We must establish a world government, federal in structure, including all the peoples of the earth.*
>
> **—Mortimer Adler**
> Former Chair of Board of Editors
> for Encyclopedia Britannica

4

The Need for a Global Legislature

*We need first and foremost
a world democracy—a government
of this planet for the people and by the people.*
—**Robert Muller**
Former UN Assistant Secretary-General

Amidst appalling inequality, nuclear proliferation, a war
on terror, and a global climate spinning out of control, international business-as-usual grinds on. Trillions of dollars in
financial transactions occur daily, untaxed and far beyond
the reach of popular control. On any given business day—as
thousands of children die of starvation—financial transactions
in developed countries, representing more than *one thousand
times* the value of all other economic transactions in the world,
flash across the screens of traders and financial analysts. This
growing power of speculative finance and investment capital is
supposedly regulated by the rules of antidemocratic institutions such as the International Monetary Fund (IMF), the
World Trade Organization (WTO) and the World Bank. It is
driven by the impersonal quest of the world's investor class for
new markets and ever-higher profits. The undeniable reality of
commerce beyond the reach of democratic global law leads us
to some stark questions:

If such "globalization without representation"[1] is permit-
ted to continue, what lays ahead for the mass of the world's
people?

What future can we expect for human rights? What fate can we expect for the "commons" of the world—the water resources, the atmosphere, the oceans, and the forests?

Are we moving toward a global dictatorship of capital, or a world democracy that ranks the needs of people higher than the search for profit?

Further, must we let the current system of global anarchy pit classes, races, and religions against one another? Or will the peoples of the world gather themselves as one global community and take control of their political destiny?

We have shown that the global issues facing humankind simply cannot be addressed without a global democratic authority—a governing structure that is legitimized by the consent of the world's peoples. We have also explained that each person is inherently a world citizen who is entitled to equal protection under global law, must be held individually accountable before world law, and possesses an intrinsic right to vote for representatives to a global democratic body.

To those with concerns that such a democratic world authority may turn into a global "tyranny of the majority," we say this: Our current course *already* is the road to a global tyranny of a wealthy and powerful minority. And we also ask: Who would you rather see make decisions that affect all of humanity: the UN General Assembly, the WTO, the World Bank, the White House—or a directly elected world parliament?

Students of government know that well-tested mechanisms already exist for controlling "majority factions" and insuring the rights of minorities in the deliberations of democratic bodies. If constitutional democracy is esteemed as the ideal for nations, how is it that representative government is not the optimal method for governing the world?

The real question is not if the world will have one government, but *what form* that government will take. Will it be a transparent, democratic, constitutional government, or will it be dominated by small groups of powerful nations and global corporations acting behind the scenes? Will it require the submission of imperial power to an objective body of world law, or will it permit great powers to veto the will of the nations at their whim? Will it allow open forums for deliberation about the global public interest, or will it stand for the unaccountable private interests of hidden global elites? Will it hide behind the mask of an obsolete national sovereignty, or will it affirm the sovereignty of the world's people? Even as you read these words, decisions are being made at the global level without humanity's consent by what might be called a *shadow* world government.

In this chapter, we will examine the proposition that moving toward the only alternative—a democratic model of world governance—may not be as difficult as one might imagine. Inspiring and useful prototypes already exist for what some have called a *global legislature,* and what others prefer to call a *world peoples' assembly* or a *world parliament.*

The grandest democratic endeavor of all time is imminent

The people of this planet don't need a "permission slip" from anyone to proclaim themselves sovereign. We can begin the great democratic experiment now. What earthly reason can justify delaying the launch of an institution that expresses our innate sovereignty?

A global parliament could be launched immediately, as an independent voice of the people—even in the absence of a global constitution or approval by the UN. And in fact, several important global organizations have already initiated significant efforts, albeit these have been largely symbolic thus far. But there are no global bureaucrats standing in the way of all possible options, blocking us with impenetrable red tape or incomprehensible regulations. When it comes to establishing world democracy, the only true limits faced by us, the sovereigns, is the degree of our passion to achieve peace and justice through one world democracy.

The point then is to simply get started; the process will gain its own momentum and will sooner or later converge with allied efforts that will inevitably culminate in the convening of a world constitutional convention—or more likely, a movement to substantially reform the UN Charter.

The ultimate goal of this grand project would be nothing less than universal planetary suffrage—generalized universal direct elections or possibly elections to world electoral colleges. We envision that the greatest political minds on the planet will convene to devise the best means to reach that final goal. We see a scenario in which, with mounting excitement, global civil society will increasingly commit itself to this essential project in humankind's evolution. Forums will appear in which historic debates will ensue over questions such as these: How should representation be apportioned? Shall there be two houses, or three? What standards must be met by a country before it can send representatives? Should the world body be parliamentary in form, or a "republic" (as in the US)?

This process of inventing a world democracy could be the most extraordinary political mission ever attempted. It could inspire millions of youths and adults throughout the world who would otherwise remain disengaged. As the world embarks on this political adventure, inspiring cultural changes will inevitably arise along with it. In his online book *World Democracy*, Troy Davis writes:

> I am certain that if we called on young volunteers to help we would witness a tidal wave of volunteers from all countries. What young person would not want to participate in the process of establishing a political system that can finally bring peace to the world? It is a once-in-a-lifetime opportunity.
>
> Seeing millions of people working at this remarkable joint project will inspire creative people of all walks of life, singers, filmmakers, writers, journalists, philosophers, spiritual leaders, and many others, and their contributions will instill momentum to the project. To conclude, the project of establishing World Democracy can be a great means of revival for civil society and popular enthusiasm. It will finally give young people an ideal and reason for hope, and give electors new faith in democracy, faith which is necessary to maintain democracy.[2]

There is nothing grandiose about putting out a call for getting under way. The idea of one world democracy makes supreme sense; this chapter demonstrates that plenty of great minds have grappled with the means and manner of getting there; indeed, the only missing ingredient is *leadership*.

Let's start by examining the European Parliament, a sitting multinational legislature that now represents the popular will of all of the peoples of the European Union.

The European Parliament is a prototype for a world parliament

The European Parliament was established in 1957, starting out as an advisory body to what was then called the European Economic Community (EEC). In the first few decades of the EEC, delegates to the Parliament were simply appointed by national parliaments. But in 1979, the citizens of all member-states were empowered to elect their representatives, which they now do every five years. With this profound change in procedure, the Parliament's prestige began to grow because of its ability to directly reflect the views of the European citizenry.

Meanwhile, new developments that began in the late 1980s turned the EEC into the world's largest trading region, as the EEC nations agreed by treaty to permit the free movement of goods, capital, people, and services across their borders.

In the next phase, the European Community was created by the Treaty of Maastricht in 1992, which led directly to the formal introduction of the European Union by a new treaty signed in 1993. Since then, Europe has seen increasing cooperation in foreign affairs as well as full economic and monetary integration, culminating in the introduction of a single currency, the euro, in 2002.

The European Parliament has evolved in parallel with Europe's economic integration, although often lagging behind. Additional democratic powers are envisioned for the Parliament in the new constitution for the EU.

Most observers project a similar pattern for the evolution of a world parliament. The experiment would likely be spurred on by the same two large forces that motivated the creation of the EU: inexorable economic integration, and the ever-present demand of civil society for improved forms of democratic participation. Seen in this light, the demand for world democracy should be on the top of the agenda of progressive activists in today's global justice movement.

Regardless of how the new world democratic union evolves, the example of the European Parliament will no doubt be a major inspiration to its framers.

Inspired citizens' efforts for global democracy have already borne fruit

Aside from the solo work of Garry Davis and his immediate followers, two non-governmental initiatives—*the peoples' assembly movement* and the ongoing efforts of the World Constitution and Parliament Association (WCPA)—are widely considered to be among the most significant grassroots efforts of global citizens for global democracy. These two exemplars represent decades of foundational and irreplaceable experience in the evolution of the struggle for a governed world. This approach to the task is what world democracy pioneer Dr. Lucile Green has called the "low road" to world government: the specialized focus on the issue of democratic participation through grassroots activism.[3]

A worldwide peoples' assembly was first proposed as far back as the 1920s during negotiations to create the League of Nations; similar calls were made at the time of the founding of the United Nations. But it required another three decades before a sustained movement had gathered around this crucial idea. The rising sentiment for grassroots global activism was especially reflected in the founding of a key organization in San Francisco in 1975, the Association of World Citizens (AWC)—now with branches in fifty nations. And San Francisco has remained the center of this movement to this day. Between 1975 and 1995, ten "World Citizen Assemblies" were held in a wide variety of locations around the world, convened by Lucille Green and by Douglas Mattern, who is currently the president of AWC. These assemblages ended where they began, in San Francisco.[4]

During this period, a milestone was reached when, during the second UN Special Session on Disarmament in 1982, a formal proposal was presented for a UN "Second

Assembly." In essence, the proposed new additional assembly would become an integral part of the UN system. Such an innovation is possible under Article 22 of the UN Charter, which states that "the General Assembly may establish such subsidiary organs as it deems necessary for the performance of its functions." It should be noted that Article 109 also provides that the Charter itself can be amended by a vote of two-thirds of the member nations along with the approval of all permanent members of the Security Council.

According to the 1982 proposal, a peoples' assembly would meet alongside the General Assembly of the UN, but seats would be allocated according to population and other measures; delegates would be non-governmental and unaffiliated with political parties. In a later elaboration of this approach, the plan for the direct election of delegates involved the nomination of candidates by community councils comprised of local branches of non-governmental and community-based organizations, rather than through national jurisdictions. These councils would then engage in public education and other activist projects that would continually feed grassroots ideas and sentiments back to their Second Assembly delegates.

A simpler proposal circulated by Lucille Green called for the direct election of a single delegate by each participating nation. Green conceived this to be a more pragmatic way to start; democratic nations would only need to add one special slate of candidates to their existing procedures for national elections. In time, this one-state one-vote approach would be amended to reflect population—and then eventually evolved toward the creation of a world legislature. But the body would initially serve in an advisory capacity to the UN, proposing issues and debating resolutions from a people's perspective.

The many Second Assembly initiatives of this era led to a series of annual conferences that culminated in 1995 at the 50th anniversary of the United Nations in San Francisco, where a symbolic "United People's Assembly" was convened. By 1997, ten follow-up "world peoples' assemblies" had met in cities like Perugia, Italy; Sao Paolo, Brazil; Wellington, New Zealand; and Los Angeles. In what appeared to be a response to these and many related efforts, in 1998 UN Secretary-General Kofi Annan called for a "Millennium People's Assembly parallel to the UN General Assembly." Thereupon, in 1999, about thirty delegations of world democracy activists from nations around the world attended the so-called Hague Appeal for Peace. This event, probably the largest peace conference ever held, convened at The Hague in the Netherlands and provided an open forum for every conceivable peace and justice organization; its program was explicitly focused on the abolition of war. Against this backdrop, people's assembly delegations organized themselves into a founding convention for a permanent global assembly. The first such assembly thereupon met in April of 2000 at the island nation of Samoa in a historic event marked by considerable fanfare. About 150 people from over fifty countries, cities, and supporting organizations met together to lay the groundwork for a permanent organization. Since then the movement has continued on a number of fronts, with much of the work focused around the San Francisco People's Assembly (SFPA)[5] and the Association of World Citizens.

The work of the peoples' assembly movement may have slowed somewhat in the post-9/11 era, though new initiatives are in the works at the time of this writing. But an important precedent has been created. The venerable history of this movement demonstrates the existence of considerable grassroots support for a functional world democracy by committed activists in nearly half the countries of the world.[6]

The other major rallying point for world democracy activists has been The Constitution for the Federation of Earth, a prototypical document that was created through the efforts of world citizens, politicians, civil society leaders, and international lawyers over a period of thirty-three years beginning in 1958. Under the leadership of the World Constitution and Parliament Association (WCPA), founded by Professor Philip Isely of Lakewood, Colorado, a series of open meetings throughout the world culminated with a provisional constitutional convention in 1968 that attracted 200 delegates from twenty-seven countries. Collaborative work on drafting a viable world constitution thereupon commenced. At the second session of what was now called the World Constituent Assembly that met at Innsbruck, Austria in 1977, an initial draft of the Constitution was debated paragraph by paragraph and the final document personally signed by those present.

This draft was then sent to all members of the UN General Assembly and to all national governments, and distributed to citizen activists worldwide for additional debate and possible revisions; the final document was completed in 1991.

Under the authority of Article 19 of this proposed Constitution, world citizens who had personally ratified it began holding "Provisional World Parliaments" to elaborate a framework of global law, which continue to this day. To date, the group has held six such meetings at locations all over the planet and a considerable body of proposed statutes has evolved.

The Earth Constitution, as it is often called, is being

promoted worldwide by the WCPA and the Institute on World Problems based in Sri Lanka and Radford, Virginia. Its many elaborate provisions describe a federation of nations, a universal bill of rights, a world administration, and a separation of powers based on the parliamentary model. The chief feature, a tricameral world parliament, is our main concern here; it is designated as the highest authority of the government. Briefly, the three houses bear the following descriptions:

1. The House of the Peoples provides for proportional representation by universal suffrage in elections from 1000 electoral districts worldwide, not unlike the model of the House of Representatives in the US Congress.

2. The House of Nations consists of one to three representatives from each nation, depending on population. This approach is weighted more toward population than the model of the US Senate.

3. The House of Counselors would be comprised of 200 members elected at large who are intended to represent the public interest of the world's people as a whole. They provide expert advice to the other two houses; vote to break deadlocks; initiate legislation or proposals that the other houses must act upon; and nominate candidates for the Presidium, a committee of five executives who head the world executive branch.[7]

In a world marked by a wide variety of cultures in widely varying stages of evolution, the innovation of providing for a House of Counselors is significant. These are the men and women most likely to represent a "worldcentric" approach to global legislation, as opposed to what is likely to be the more parochial points of view of the representatives elected to the other two houses—some of whom may even represent ethnocentric or even tribal points of view. The structure of the

WCPA's Constitution appears to ensure that the members of the key echelon of leadership for the planet represent the highest possible evolution of consciousness on the planet.[8]

The movement around the WCPA, including the successive meetings of its Provisional World Parliament, represents a substantive expression of global democracy at work. Writes Dr. Glen Martin, current Secretary-General of the WCPA: "We are all already citizens of the Earth Federation. In the darkness of these times, we know that tomorrow is too late, and the time is now. A new dawn is rising for the world. Liberation for humanity is at hand. Citizens of the world unite!"[9]

A world parliament could be launched as an autonomous body

Another workable approach to creating a world parliament or legislature has been circulated in prestigious foreign affairs journals in recent years by two eminent thinkers: Richard Falk, professor emeritus of international law at Princeton University and author of dozens of books, and Andrew Strauss, professor of international law at Widener University School of Law. We examine this plan more closely than other initiatives because it has recently garnered attention at the highest levels of today's foreign policy establishment.

The vision of Falk and Strauss is not encumbered by its association with a particular constitutional framework (as is the case of the movement piloted by the WCPA), or by an affiliation with the UN system (as with the peoples' assembly movement). Instead they envision that a world parliament could be established, even within this decade, as an autonomous body and a rallying point for new efforts to develop a world constitution or a reformed UN.

However, if not arising from within an existing

institutional structure, who then would initiate the global parliament, and how? Ideally, a core group of national governments would lend the prestige of their support. Falk and Strauss write that a people's world forum could best be launched as a special initiative by such a pioneering group of democratic governments, supported especially by a worldwide grassroots campaign led by NGOs: "As few as twenty to thirty geographically, culturally, and economically diverse countries would be enough to credibly launch this experiment in global democracy."[10] A vanguard group of this sort would create an experimental body about the size of the European Parliament —that is, if in fact NGOs could be persuaded to do most of the organizing and persuading, and if in addition a sufficient number of visionary politicians could be recruited from many nations.

It is a fact that a myriad of NGOs and numerous other business, labor, media, human rights, cultural, and religious organizations already engage in activities whose scope is international. All such groups constitute "a highly visible globalized citizenry that now has the capacity, perhaps with the help of some forward-looking governments, to organize such an assembly."

Falk and Strauss indicate that the lack of strong governmental support would not be the most decisive factor in this scenario, and would not be a legal requirement. (It should be noted that the WCPA's appeals over many decades to national governments were largely ignored.) So what other steps could bring this assembly into being? This is what the professors wrote in the International Herald Tribune:

> Perhaps the most effective initial move would be to issue an appeal endorsed by moral authority figures (religious leaders, Nobel Peace Prize laureates) that calls on the peoples of the world to bring about such an assembly.

> If well-executed, this appeal would probably succeed in raising needed organizing funds.
>
> As a second stage, meetings could be arranged throughout the world with the goal of forming a citizens' committee that could organize and administer global elections. A voting formula based upon one person, one vote would probably be acceptable and fairest. Elections could then be held, monitored by respected observers. . . . Global voter rolls would have to be generated. A system of campaign finance and other election rules would need to be established, and attempts to manipulate or undermine elections would have to be effectively guarded against.[11]

If all this could be accomplished, the process of electing the very first delegates to this body would be a momentous step. From there, one can imagine that the self-expression of the people's inherent sovereignty would naturally and dynamically unfold. Each election cycle in a democratic nation pushes forward the evolution of that nation's civic culture as it is expressed through polls, punditry, political parties, a watchdog press, political campaigns, and all the rest. One can expect the same to occur in the ongoing articulation of a world citizens' global political culture, once initiated.

In time, a distinctive institutional identity would emerge—the people's world parliament! Allowed for the first time to participate in creating global law, one might also imagine the exuberance of an organized world citizenry and how it would become institutionally committed to the parliament and invested in its success. Starting from humble beginnings, the global assembly would become an unstoppable force, expressing the long pent-up demand for the political enfranchisement of the world's people.

In the Falk and Strauss model, the global parliamentary assembly would at first follow the example of the European

Parliament; its function would initially be advisory. But once in place, it probably would gradually increase in influence and reputation as the needs of an increasingly interdependent world come to the fore through the voices of its enfranchised citizens. One can only imagine the huge array of citizen groups and NGOs that would line up to petition the global parliament to pass resolutions supportive of their positions.

But what would happen, in the meantime, to those elites and business groups who brought us the IMF, the WTO, and the World Bank, and who stand to lose power because of the democratization of the planet? This is how Falk and Strauss answer:

> Those opposed to the policy preferences of these citizen groups, whether industrial lobbies, labor unions, states or other citizen groups, would likely be unwilling to concede to their opponents the legitimacy of the only popularly elected global body. Instead, they would likely come to participate as well. It is even possible that nationalistic critics and policymakers hostile to global democracy would be inclined to participate and put forth their own views. As groups found in the parliament a transnational civic space in which to work out their differences, the center of political gravity could subtly shift in the parliament's favor.[12]

A further step would be that of expanding the parliament's membership. Falk and Strauss believe that just as soon as the world parliament begins functioning, citizen groups from countries around the world would themselves exert pressure on their governments to join in the venture. Eventually, a critical mass of membership would be reached. Even the most authoritarian governments would at some point find it embarrassing to deny their citizens the right to be represented.

According to the authors, one possible outcome of this unfolding would be the incorporation of the parliament into the UN system, instituted as a "lower house" of a "World

Congress" alongside the General Assembly; this would make it part of a bicameral legislative system that would supplement or hopefully supplant the Security Council. Another path would be to link this independent effort toward world democracy with an independent call for a world constitutional convention, perhaps with delegates from the world parliament.

Any act of launching a global parliament would give hope and inspiration to the world's people; it would also begin to offer aggrieved groups a genuine alternative to terrorism or civil war. The authors state:

> Those alienated by perceived injustices or by global silence about their grievances would no longer have to choose between surrender and the adoption of desperate tactics. Instead, they would have a legitimate international forum in which they could at least be heard and perhaps find enough support to achieve peaceful redress. Citizens would be able to stand for office, champion candidates and form coalitions to lobby the parliament, a process that would bring those with diverse or opposing views into a give-and-take setting that would improve the chances for compromise and reconciliation. Those whose views did not prevail would likely be more inclined to accept defeat out of a belief in the fairness of the process, and with an understanding that they could continue to press their cause on future occasions. . . . Of course, the Osama bin Ladens of the planet will never accept the legitimacy of a global parliamentary process. But their ability to attract a significant following might well be substantially diminished by the presence of such an institution, especially if the legitimate grievances of peoples around the world were being consistently addressed with an eye toward the realization of global justice and the promotion of the rule of law.[13]

A *constitutional* global democracy is needed now

It is worth repeating that a world parliament could operate at first in an advisory capacity, prior to the creation of a world constitution or a reformed UN. It was many years before the European Parliament was formally incorporated into the European Union, which then conferred upon it the power to write binding legislation through a constitution that was proposed decades after the advisory parliament was created. In the same way, the advisory world legislature would at a later point converge with—and derive final legitimacy from—efforts to create a new constitution for a federal world government, and would be further shaped by this larger endeavor. One can imagine that this "latter-day" constitution (or UN Charter review conference) would extract the best lessons learned from the ongoing experiment of the global parliament and blend these with what the planet's finest minds would devise for a new world executive and judiciary system.

There would be much to draw from. Many proposals for a constitution for a world federation exist aside from the WCPA, many of which were first promulgated in the golden age of thought about world government in the late 1940s and 1950s. The first and boldest was the Preliminary Draft of a World Constitution (1948), created by the University of Chicago's Committee to Frame a World Constitution, an effort that was led by the eminent scholar and educator Robert Maynard Hutchins and professors Mortimer Adler and G. A. Borgese. Another was enunciated in *World Peace through World Law* (1958), a detailed book by Grenville Clark and Louis B. Sohn, two Harvard professors, which essentially offered a substantive reform of the United Nations Charter. These two draft constitutions span the range between "maximal" and "minimal" concepts, respectively. The maximalist approach would vest the world government with broad powers to achieve peace and justice; the minimalist approach would restrict it primarily to powers involving the maintenance of international security. Like any government, a global government is a balancing act; it should be set up so that it is not too powerful (thus avoiding tyranny) and not too weak (thus avoiding ineffectiveness).

In addition to the Chicago committee's draft and the Clark-Sohn plan, there have been well over fifty other model world constitutions. To this day the best known among these is the Constitution for the Federation of Earth, noted earlier, which has two key advantages: It has been translated into twenty-two languages and widely distributed, and it was created through a process of four constituent assemblies of diverse membership over a period of twenty-three years, lending it a democratic authenticity that other proposed constitutions lack.

There have also been countless proposals for UN reform, though none quite on the scale of the Clark-Sohn plan. These include the Binding Triad proposal of Richard Hudson, and the fourteen-point plan of the Campaign for UN Reform. These various proposals show, at the least, that a lawful federation of the modern world is conceivable, and most could easily serve as draft negotiating documents for a realistic program of political action.

In a world federation, the issue of democratic representation is considered one of the most challenging problems. Should representation be proportional to population—the strictly democratic principle? This would obviously give predominance to poorer, more populous, and less "politically experienced" countries. We've seen how WCPA's Constitution addresses this matter. Or should representation be weighted somehow to make active participation more attractive to the world's great powers? Clark and Sohn advocated that the UN

General Assembly should be reorganized according to a system of weighted representation, scaled with respect to population, wealth, education, and traditional great-power ranking. Thus the US, Russia, China, and India were to each be allocated thirty delegates; mid-sized powers such as Britain, France, West Germany, and Japan, sixteen delegates; smaller nations, eight; and so on down through seven steps to the smallest states, which jointly would be granted one delegate. This scheme produced a total of 625 world representatives. Clark and Sohn urged that the representatives be directly elected by the people wherever possible, so that they develop a sense of responsibility to their constituents instead of to national governments; elsewhere, appointment by parliaments or national monarchs would have to be allowed.

The Chicago committee proposed a rather different scheme—more on the "republican" model of the US Constitution. It provides for regional popular elections and nine electoral colleges, thus eliminating the cumbersome weighting scheme. Representatives to the world legislature would be elected by all the electoral colleges sitting in plenary session. Through this technique, each representative would, in principle, reflect the public interest of the whole world. In stark contrast with other plans, the Chicago approach would result in a world legislature of only ninety-nine delegates!

More recently, Professor Joseph E. Schwartzberg's widely distributed approach developed in conjunction with the Institute for Global Policy, a think tank operated by the World Federalist Movement, has devised a system of weighted voting that could be used by a reformed General Assembly of the UN. This system uses a mathematical formula based on population, financial contribution to the UN, and membership. This system, if in place today, would give the US a weighted vote of 9.1 percent, China 7.7 percent, Japan 7.3 percent, India 6.0 percent, Germany 3.8 percent, etc. Schwartzberg also made the following suggestions as to the minimal requirements for launching a global assembly:

(a) At least twenty nations must agree to the basic conditions.

(b) Nations from at least four continents must be included.

(c) Participating nations must account for at least 15 percent of the world's population.

(d) Participating nations must account for at least 15 percent of the UN's budget.[14]

Whatever the technical arrangements might turn out to be, the almost sacred work of creating a global democratic body is the best insurance that humankind could ever devise against global crises such as terrorism, world wars, and environmental destruction. It will be a forum for permanent political dialogue of all peoples and for the adoption of laws that reflect their sovereign will. As the one world democracy evolves, old notions of an inevitable "clash of civilizations" will become a relic of the past. Christian, Hindu, Buddhist, Muslim, and the secular-minded Westerners alike will grow to treasure this forum for peaceful deliberation. And for the first time in history, it will elevate world commerce and global politics by putting these under the aegis of enforceable global law.

A World People's Assembly [could] become an integral
part of a reformed and democratized United Nations,
modified and strengthened to defend the common interest
of humankind so aptly stated in the Preamble to the
UN Charter. The time to begin is at hand.
—Lucille Green

5

The War
System and the
Wisdom of Federation

*I represent a party which does not yet exist—
the party of . . . civilization. . . . There will come
from it first a United States of Europe, and
then a United States of the World.*
—Victor Hugo

World federation is a form of international organization in which the nations of the world *share power* in order to achieve common goals—chiefly the abolition of war. As we will see in this chapter, a federation of nations is the political technique by which the scourge of the war system shall finally be removed from the face of the earth.

In our discussions of global governance, we have been assuming the supremacy of the federal model of power sharing. Federation appears to be the only viable option among several possible approaches to integrating national sovereignty within a larger global structure. There is genius and wisdom in the federation approach.

Inspired world-citizen activists will one day form the crucial constituency for a global government, but our elected national leaders will also have a key role. It is they who must some day play the courageous central role of surrendering a part of their nations' sovereignty in order to create the *federation* of nations that will be the political backbone of the government of humankind.

The minimalist approach to world government best illustrates the beauty of federation; by joining the federation, member-nations agree to forever abolish war as a method for solving problems between them. They will do this by simply delegating the work of maintenance of international peace and security to the executive branch of the new federation. The world federation will create global courts (as described in its constitution) whose initial purpose will be the binding adjudication of all international disputes, thus replacing war and terrorism as an institution for solving such difficulties. National and local disputes would still be left to national and local authorities—with the exception that the minimalist world federation would have certain limited jurisdiction over civil wars within states.

The world legislature would likely be the supreme organization operating under the auspices of the federation. It would represent the will of the world's people in regard to those matters of global importance that are delegated to the world body by the member-nations.

The war system
has an insidious effect

We have already demonstrated that war will never cease as long as nations cling to the illusive notion of unlimited national sovereignty, and unless they delegate their war-making powers to a super-sovereign entity. In recent times, we have also seen convincing evidence that virtually all terrorism is state-sponsored or is surreptitiously supported by the state apparatus of rogue states that regard terror as one means of exercising their supposed sovereign right to make war. We are proposing an end to war and terrorism by the voluntary surrender to a world federation of this supposed "right" of nations to use force in international affairs.

A world federation would maintain order only by deploying a world police force; like federal marshals in the US, world marshals would enforce the laws of the federation as these apply to individuals (including individual terrorists), not entire states. Even in the case of a rogue state run amuck, the enforcement action of the federation is brought against individual leaders of the state, not against the entire nation and its people. This is obviously rather different from the use of force implied in the military action of nations against one another or in the case of civil wars within nations. Police are trained to use the minimum force against individuals as is required to restore lawful order or to make an arrest of a person or persons while avoiding injury to innocent bystanders; by contrast, military action is a maximum force based on the survival imperatives of a nation or subgroup within a nation, and is designed to take control of a general area with less regard for innocent civilians. In simpler words, police arrest individuals—they don't drop bombs on nations. Inside federations like that of the United States, police force is the only force used for all domestic law enforcement short of civil war. It is in this sense that it can truly be said that the eventual elimination of the use of military force anywhere in the world is the aim of a world federation.

We may wax eloquent on this thesis, but let us pause to consider the meaning of these visionary ideas from the standpoint of a newly elected liberal prime minister of, say, a democratic nation in Asia or Africa. This leader of ours, of course, must deal with the world as it is *today*. He or she must operate in the absence of the security protections of a federation of nations about which we luxuriously theorize. His or her predicament, presented below, shows how difficult and how crucial it will be to *first* abolish the global war system if one is to truly liberate this politician for effective service to his country.

Sitting for the first time at the center of a national government no doubt brings a stark clarity of mind to our imaginary prime minister. As he begins to look around, he soon perceives a myriad of dangers staring back at him, including international terrorism, a proliferation of WMDs on his continent, neighboring countries ruled by dictators, an impotent United Nations, and incursions by predatory forces of economic globalization. Suddenly, this person's constitutional responsibility to defend the homeland in the face of these threats begins to look somewhat more solemn. His original intent to pursue and fund liberal domestic programs to address the needs of his people starts to seem less important.

And what are the rules of the international system into which the prime minister has been thrust?

It quickly becomes clear to him that the first rule is this: The threat of war will always exist. He wonders if there is a force that can guarantee the nation absolute safety. Indeed there is none. "We must rely on our own military prowess," he realizes. "War can and will break out, and with it comes the possibility of defeat. With defeat come the loss of sovereignty and the likelihood of economic ruin. Defeat could even mean the destruction of the nation. That's one of the rules of this system. If it is not some war fomented by one of our neighbors, or by the imperial United States, terrorists could infiltrate our country and wreak havoc."

What national leader would want to be blamed for such things? Certainly not our prime minister.

One can then ask: What is the prime minister's most rational response to the ever-present threat of a contest of force and the looming consequences of defeat? Clear thinking dictates that preparations for war and defense against all possible forms of aggression must become his top priority.

Our leader now realizes that every aspect of national life must be evaluated in terms of the capacity to fight and win a war, if and when such measures become necessary. Planning for this exigency should not be seen as "militarism" on his part. It is only fair to see it as reasonable behavior, given the rules of the war system he cannot control.

Every day, generals in the armed forces are on hand in the national palace to remind the prime minister of his grim responsibilities. Indeed, these generals appear to be sane and logical people, genuine realists. They are professionals whose lifework is the mastery of the rules of the war system.

This example can suffice to show how the system works, and how it creates a lockstep mentality in all of the players. In the final analysis, it is this anarchic system that is to blame for our warlike ways on this planet—not any individual leader, and certainly not the presence of certain weapons or the greed of the industrialists who manufacture and ship them. With a problem as serious as warfare in the age of WMDs, we must be disciplined enough to distinguish true causes from mere effects.

The war system is toxic in each country

We should not be surprised then if our prime minister, once a liberal democrat, now starts subordinating industrial, agricultural, welfare, and other domestic policies to the imperative of national defense. If mounting a proper defense seems to require educating more scientists, then it would only be rational that he ask the legislature to subsidize their education. If victory in war seems to depend on the size of the population, then we should not be surprised if he starts encouraging large families. If neighbors or dominant nations have WMDs, we shouldn't be stunned if he seeks to secretly build a national stockpile of suitable WMDs. If adversaries are seen as wily and deceitful, then we shouldn't blame the prime minister for expanding the budget of his intelligence agencies.

"Our liberal legislators who are urging cooperation with other countries should be highly suspect," says the prime minister to himself. A treaty with a neighbor may create some advantages, but how can one ensure that some tyrant doesn't come to power inside that country and simply ignore the treaty? "In the end you can't trust those other countries," the prime minister whispers to his wife one night.

Soon the prospect of manipulating and even lying to rival nations, through "diplomacy," begins to make supreme sense to him. "No doubt the other side has thought of using deception," says one of his generals. "And if not, it's best to deploy it first. After all, these treaties cannot be relied upon!"

It has become easier now to justify shrewdness, deception, weapons stockpiling, and a general fortress mentality. If the prime minister does not listen to the logic that supports these conclusions, perhaps the threat of a military coup can keep him in line. The military men know the requirements of the system, after all.

Indeed, in the war system, promoting national security is what counts; the morality of international relations is almost irrelevant. National power is the basis of getting what you want and the security you need. Everything else must be secondary to that. It's nobody's fault, but everyone is to blame.

If war does break out, the logic of the war system then reaches its apex. Killing, destruction, and deception of the enemy become supreme virtues. Dropping a nuclear weapon on one or two of their cities may seem to be the very height of military virtue. This gives a reason for our imaginary leader to do what he can to get his own nukes.

The upshot is this: Wars that end in terrible destruction are not just happenstance. They don't just occur because of a few whimsical leaders. *War is the central feature of the system.* War is the court of last resort in a world of anarchy; all nations must be prepared to face warfare or they will perish.

It should be obvious that the next step in this narrative is domestic repression. Our prime minister now decides that, in the interest of national security, it will be necessary to hide the truth about the nation's defense policies from his people. A secret "black budget" must be created in order to fund biological and nuclear weapons development programs. The legislature simply cannot be trusted with this strategic decision, he realizes. It is too inwardly focused, too riddled with amateur political thinkers—even members of his own party. Furthermore, young people must be taught militaristic values, and the importance of subordinating their rights to those in authority. This will prepare them for the confrontations to come.

"It is not hard to see," writes world federalist scholar Ronald J. Glossop whose book *World Federation?* is the source of the above argument, that "[the] anarchic international system encourages a 'militaristic' kind of expediency which is directly opposed to the concern for justice, human rights, and open discussion of policy options on which democratic governance is founded." A toxic cult of militarism that feeds off and responds to the war system almost directly confronts the democratic sympathies of the general population, acting as a brake on the forward evolution of national life. (For vivid examples, consider the recent history of nations such as Chile, Israel, Burma, Turkey, or even the United States.)

It may seem to the progressive forces of a country that the kind of militarism we have been describing is excessive, even paranoid. But we have analyzed the dilemma faced by our prime ministers, as seen through his eyes. He is being called an aggressive warmonger by the leftist forces within his country, but the truth is that he has little choice. If he strikes a conciliatory attitude toward other countries, the results could be disastrous. If he listens to the peace activists and cuts the military budget, the country could be coerced into unacceptable agreements. Regardless of his own personal sympathies, he and all other elected leaders on this planet must dance to the tune of the war system until the system has been replaced.

World federation is the solution to the war system

Each phase in the evolution of political sovereignty must contend with what we have called the "scaffolding stages" of the previous developments in political organization. This is true because human loyalties, once mobilized to deal with the stark necessities of one age, are hard to change as a new era approaches.

For example, the loyalty to a tribal chief that once made possible the survival of the tribe makes very difficult the evolution of the "supertribe"—the nation. (One can see this, for example, in the conflict between tribal sheiks in Afghanistan and the central government in Kabul.) Likewise, the same loyalty that makes possible the evolution of the nation-state, patriotism and "rational" militarism, vastly complicates the evolution of the government of all humankind.

Even with this dose of realism, it still remains the case that "international law" can never bring permanent peace to mankind; the logic of the war system is far more compelling. Collective security measures are a step in the right direction; an international police force can prevent or contain many minor wars, as the UN has done at times. But the UN as it is currently structured will never be effective in preventing major wars, ending great-power conflicts like the ruinous Cold War, or stopping unilateral conquests by a superpower, such as the US invasion of Iraq in 2003.

In the end, peace will not come to this planet until every so-called sovereign nation surrenders its power to make war into the hands of a representative government of all humankind. Political sovereignty is innate to the peoples of the world. When all the peoples of earth one day create a world government, they have the right and the power to make such a government SOVEREIGN, and when such a representative or democratic world power controls the world's land, air, and naval forces, we will have an end to war.

These memorable words were spoken on October 19, 1999 by Walter Cronkite, on the occasion of winning the Norman Cousins Global Governance Award:

> ...We must strengthen the United Nations as a first step toward a world government patterned after our own government with a legislature, executive and judiciary, and police to enforce its international laws and keep the peace.
>
> To do that, of course, we Americans will have to yield up some of our sovereignty. That would be a bitter pill. It would take a lot of courage, a lot of faith in the new order.
>
> But the American colonies did it once and brought forth one of the most nearly perfect unions the world has ever seen.
>
> ...We cannot defer this responsibility to posterity. Time will not wait. Democracy, civilization itself, is at stake. Within the next few years we must change the basic structure of our

global community from the present anarchic system of war and ever more destructive weaponry to a new system governed by a democratic UN federation.

...In their almost miraculous insight, the founders of our country invented 'federalism,' a concept rooted in the rights of the individual. Our federal system guarantees a maximum of freedom but provides it in a framework of law and justice.

Today we must develop federal structures on a global level. We need a system of enforceable world law—a democratic federal world government—to deal with world problems.

World federalism arose in response to World War II

The idea of creating a political union of states in order to abolish war may be traced back for centuries—back to Woodrow Wilson, Immanuel Kant, and even to the poet Dante. However, until the collapse of the League of Nations in the 1930s that led to the horrors of WWII, most proposals of international union were not federalist. The great German philosopher Kant, for instance, spoke only of a confederation of free and independent states. President Wilson's own proposals for world peace were far from advocating world federation.

It turns out that the modern doctrine of a global federation has its roots in surprisingly recent developments, despite the longstanding success of the federal union of the United States of America, the prototypical example of a successful federation. World federalism arose in the 1940s as the most brilliant response to the hard lessons of the first part of the twentieth century.

The search for radical new solutions began in the late 1930s with the ignominious collapse of the League of Nations. Many argued, as did Clarence Streit in the famous book *Union Now!* (1939), that the League failed because it had tragically preserved the principle of the absolute national sovereignty of states. Streit was one of the first to show that the transfer of a portion of national sovereignty was necessary to prevent war. He argued that the principle of federal government had already proven its ability to create peace as illustrated in the constitutions of the United States of America, the United Kingdom, and other nations whose constitutions were based on a federation of smaller states. Streit's proposals were, however, limited to a federation of democratic nations.

It was none other than Albert Einstein who was a primary influence for the next phase of the evolution of the idea of world federalism. It happened that, shortly after the US bombed Hiroshima and Nagasaki and in the midst of the horror of those events, journalists visited Einstein and asked for his opinion on the question of world peace after Hiroshima. His reply was unequivocal: We need a world government. Einstein then urged the journalists to read a new book by Emery Reves entitled *The Anatomy of Peace*. With Einstein's endorsement, this book became an instantaneous bestseller. The ideas in this book were enormously influential in launching the "one world" movement of the late 1940s.

Reves was a journalist who directed a large press service in Europe and New York, before and during World War II. He provided the first articulation of world federalism as we know it today. The extensive excerpt from this text below references the early days of the debate over the adoption of the UN Charter early in 1945.

> There is only one method that can create security against destruction by the atomic bomb. This is the same method that gives the states of New York and California (non-producers of the atomic bomb) security against being erased from the surface of the earth by the states of Tennessee and

New Mexico (producers of the atomic bomb). This security is real. It is the security given by a common sovereign order of law. Outside of that, any security is but an illusion.

Many of the scientists who released atomic energy, frightened by the consequences of this new force, warn us of the dangers that will result if several sovereign states possess atomic weapons, and urge control of it by the United Nations Security Council.

But what is the United Nations Security Council, except "several sovereign states"?

What is the reality of the Security Council beyond the reality of the sovereign nation-states that compose it?

What matters if the American secretary of state, the Soviet foreign commissar, and His Majesty's foreign secretary meet as members of the United Nations Security Council or outside that organization in a "Conference of Foreign Ministers"? In either case they are but the sworn representatives of three conflicting sovereign nation-states; in either case the final decisions rest with Washington, London and Moscow. These representatives can only arrive at agreements or treaties and are without power to create law applicable to the individuals of their respective nation-states.

Many of those who realize the inadequacy of the San Francisco organization [i.e., the United Nations Organization, or UNO] feel that the people must not be disillusioned, that their faith in the organization must not be destroyed.

If that faith is not justified, it must be destroyed. It is criminal to mislead the people and teach them to rely on a false hope.

The pathetic defenders argue that the UNO is all we have and we should be practical and start from what we have. A reasonable suggestion. It is scarcely possible to start from anywhere except from where we are. If a man has measles, no matter what he plans to do, he must start with the measles. But this does not mean that measles is an asset, a welcome condition, and that he could not do things better without measles. The mere fact of having something does not automatically make it valuable.

The San Francisco Charter is a multilateral treaty. That and nothing else. Each party to it can withdraw the moment it desires, and war alone can force the member-states to fulfill their obligations under the treaty. For several thousand years man has given innumerable chances to treaty structures between sovereign power units to demonstrate that they can prevent war. With the possibility of atomic war facing us, we cannot risk reliance upon a method that has failed miserably hundreds of times and never succeeded once.

A realization that this method can never prevent war is the first condition of peace. Law and only law can bring peace among men; treaties never can.

We can never arrive at a legal order by amending a treaty structure. To realize the task before us, the heated debates of Hamilton, Madison, and Jay in Philadelphia should be read and reread in every home and every school. They demonstrated that the Articles of Confederation (based on the same principles as the United Nations Organization) could not prevent war between the states, that amendment of these articles could not solve the problem…establishing an overall federal government with power to legislate, apply and execute law on individuals in the United States. That was the only remedy then and it is the only remedy now.

Such criticism of the United Nations Organization may shock people who have been persuaded that the UNO is an instrument for maintaining peace.

The San Francisco league is not a first step toward a universal legal order. To change from a treaty basis to law is one step, one operation, and it is impossible to break it into parts or fractions. This decision has to be made and the operation carried out at one time. There is no "first step" toward world government. World government is the first step.

Some remark patronizingly: "But this is idealism. Let us be realistic, let us make the San Francisco organization work."

What is idealism? And what is realism? Is it realistic to believe that treaties—which have been tried again and again and have always failed—will now miraculously work? And is it idealistic to believe that law—which has always succeeded wherever and whenever it was applied—will continue to work?

Every time our foreign ministers or the heads of our governments meet and decide not to decide, hurry to postpone, and commit themselves to no commitments, the official heralds proclaim jubilantly to the universe: "This is a hopeful beginning." "This is a first step in the right direction."

We are always beginning . . . We never continue, never carry on, complete or conclude. We never take a second step or—God forbid—a third step. Our international life is composed of an unending sequence of beginnings that don't begin, of first steps that lead nowhere. When are we going to tire of this game?

It is of utmost importance to look at these things in their proper perspective. We must reject the exhortations of reactionaries who say: "Of course, world government is the ultimate goal. But we can't get it now. We must proceed slowly, step by step."

World government is not an "ultimate goal" but an immediate necessity. In fact, it has been overdue since 1914. The convulsions of the past decades are the clear symptoms of a dead and decaying political system.

Whether the change from treaty structure to a legal order takes place independently of the United Nations Organization or within it is irrelevant. To amend the San Francisco Charter—if that is the road we choose—we will have to rewrite it so drastically to get what we need that nothing of the document will remain except the two opening words: "Chapter One." The change has to come about in our minds, in our outlook. Once we know what we want, it makes no difference whether the reform is carried out on top of the Eiffel Tower, in the bleachers of the Yankee Stadium, or on the floor of the United Nations General Assembly.

The stumbling block to transforming the San Francisco league into a governmental institution is the Charter's basic conception expressed in the first phrase of the first chapter: "Members are the states."

This makes the charter a multilateral treaty. No amendment of the text can alter that fact until the very foundation is changed to the effect that the institution will have direct relationship, not with states but with individuals.

But—argue the defenders of the Charter—the preamble says, "We the Peoples of the United Nations. . . ." Suppose someone publishes a proclamation opening, "I, the Emperor of China. . . ." Would this make him the Emperor of China? Such an action would more probably land him in a lunatic asylum than on the throne of China. "We, the people. . . ." —these symbolic words of democratic government—do not belong in the San Francisco Charter. Their use in the preamble is in total contradiction to everything else in it, and only historians will be able to decide whether they were used from lack of knowledge or lack of honesty. The simple truth requires that "We, the Peoples. . . ." in the preamble of the Charter be accurately read: "We, the High Contracting Powers. . . ."

The most vulgar of all objections, of course, is the meaningless assertion made by so many "public figures": "The people are not yet ready for world federation."

One can only wonder how they know. Have they themselves ever advocated world federation? Do they themselves believe in it? Have they ever tried to explain to the people what makes war and what is the mechanism of peace in human society? And, after having understood the problem, have the people rejected the solution and decided they did not want peace by law and government but preferred war by national sovereignty? Until this happens, no one has the right to pretend he knows what the people are ready for. Ideals always seem premature—until they become obsolete. Everybody has a perfect right to say that he does not believe in federal world government and does not want it. But without having faith in it and without having tried it, nobody has the right to preclude the decision of the people.[1]

Federation is radically different from confederation

At this juncture, let us revisit and once again clearly distinguish a confederation of "High Contracting Parties," as Reves mockingly puts it above, from a federation of states that genuinely represents "We the people of planet earth."

A confederation is nothing more nor less than a voluntary association of states as may be reflected in a treaty, a convention, or an organization such as the UN or NATO. States are still understood to be sovereign, though in fact by joining a confederation—just as in entering into treaties and alliances—they accept minor limitations on their freedom of action. At the same time, in accordance with "international law," states retain the right to reject the confederation's recommendations. In addition, member-states enforce the confederation's decisions only by means of their own national laws, or by the *principle of collective security.*

The great weakness of confederation is vividly shown in this notion of collective security, the primary mode of enforcement used by the United Nations. While it is true that collective security is an improvement on the unbridled national adventurism of the past, its solutions involve the very cumbersome imposition of sanctions and ultimately war on the entire people of the offending state itself—rather than the operation of enforceable law applied to individuals.

That explains in large part why the UN's efforts to prevent war have been so ineffective and counterproductive. At the UN's founding, a debate arose about this notion of imposing economic sanctions or waging war as the UN's favored mode of punishment of violators of international law. Understandably, the great powers and many other nations objected to this proposed enforcement mechanism as being indiscriminate and onerous. But the solution adopted was a bizarre compromise: These framers of the UN Charter included debilitating protections against the egregious effects of its own enforcement mechanism! They found themselves resorting to the technique of unanimity—and the option of a veto for the largest powers—in the very council that they envisioned for making these enforcement decisions.

It is especially the veto power of the large states that vitiates the logic of the whole UN system. It prevents enforcement in the cases that really matter, and it establishes a psychological climate of inaction and powerlessness that has led many around the world to reject the entire concept of global solutions to global problems.

It is little wonder that mainstream politicians within the United States and elsewhere have turned away from the UN, and for several decades have been in search of other solutions to issues of war and peace. It is not only contempt for international restraints on America's ability to act that drives this search; this sentiment represents a genuine frustration with the way that the system itself generates poor decisions and ineffective enforcement by anyone's measure.

Historically, the collective security mechanism of the United Nations has been exercised in significant ways only twice, with questionable results: first, when the United Nations deployed military forces against North Korea in 1950 in an action dominated by the US and, later, in the Gulf War with its US-led alliance of nations that attacked Iraq in 1991.

In the years since its founding, UN "peacekeeping" forces (lightly armed for patrol and observation purposes only) have also conducted a few dozen valuable operations designed to stabilize cease-fire lines and to encourage negotiations, but they have had little impact on the 200 wars that have occurred since 1945, in which an estimated 30 million have perished.

The benefits of federation are many

In the final analysis, the nations of earth have never possessed real sovereignty; they never have had a sovereignty that could protect them from the ravages and devastation of regional or world wars. In the creation of a global government of humankind, the nations are not giving up sovereignty so much as they are actually creating a real, bona fide, and lasting world sovereignty which will be fully able to protect them from all war. Toward this end, world federation offers a simple and elegant formula: Local affairs will be handled by local governments; national affairs, by national governments; and international affairs will be administered by the world government.

World citizens—the constituents of a global government who will one day elect a world legislature—will enjoy far more liberty under the government of humankind. Today Americans are taxed and regulated almost oppressively because of the onerous requirements of the war system and a military-industrial complex that has spun out of control. Much of this interference with individual liberties is based on a rational response to the "rules" of the war system, but this rollback of civil liberties will vanish when our government sees the wisdom of entrusting its sovereignty as regards to war-making into the hands of global government.

Under a global government all national groups will be afforded a real opportunity to realize and enjoy the personal liberties of genuine democracy. The fallacy of absolute national sovereignty will have ended. With global regulation of money and trade will come a new era of worldwide peace, as has already been seen in microcosm in the European Union and other successful federations. In time there will even be the hope that religions with a liberal, tolerant, and "worldcentric" viewpoint may come to dominate the cultural landscape. Such would be a welcome change from the proliferation of funda-mentalist variants of Christianity and Islam that seem to be on the rise across the world as ordinary people desperately attempt to grapple with the spiritual impact of global anarchy and unregulated economic globalization.

Which approach sounds most realistic? A patchwork reform of the UN that leaves in place the framework of a confederation—or a world federation? World federalists say that it is they who wish to extend the rule of law, who are the realists. They maintain that those who put their faith in a league of sovereign states are the delusional ones.

Paradoxically, under today's system of collective security mixed with international anarchy—a system ostensibly contrived to protect national sovereignty—the nation-state as such is actually *undermined*. It is a world federation above all that will preserve what is unique and culturally essential about nations, while transcending and leaving behind those characteristics of national sovereignty that offer nothing of value to the evolution of humankind.

A federation of nations, in which countries are united to a significant degree, but maintain much separateness, is the most logical arrangement. Such a federation would provide for different levels of government. Under the American system of federal government, states and cities are allowed to make certain independent decisions. For example, gambling is legal in Nevada but illegal in most other states. However, the right to make war and enter into international agreements is reserved for the national government. A federation shares power with the different levels of government, in contrast to a unitary state, in which all decisions are made by a central authority. Federal global government would simply complete the American system of federal government by adding the missing highest level.

The goal of a world federation is international unity, not uniformity. However, once a nation joined the global government, it would give up some of its right to independent action. For instance, it would not have the right to secede, just as in the 1860s the southern states did not have the right to secede from the US and were forced back into the union. The obligations of government are never voluntary. This is the difference between a confederation, in which obligations are voluntary, and a government, in which they are binding.

World federalism is in fact the most acceptable way, in an interdependent world, by which legitimate features of national and local sovereignty can be preserved; they *must* be preserved, under a world federation, as sources of law that are better adapted to national and local circumstances. In the final analysis, world federation is the only acceptable form of international organization that is strong enough to abolish war, yet not so strong as to endanger the political and cultural diversity of mankind. Federation is the wise approach to global governance. "Unity in diversity" will undoubtedly be the watchwords of the future federation of all nations.

> *Mankind's desire for peace can be realized*
> *only by the creation of a world government.*
> *With all my heart I believe that the world's*
> *present system of sovereign nations can only*
> *lead to barbarism, war, and inhumanity.*
> —Albert Einstein

6

How Do We Create a World Government?

*Government is the thing. Law is the thing. Not
brotherhood, not international cooperation,
not security councils that can stop war only by
waging it. . . . Where does security lie, anyway—
security against the thief, the murderer? In
brotherly love? Not at all. It lies in government.*

—E.B. White

The historic meetings in San Francisco at the close of
WWII that led to the signing of the UN Charter created an
unprecedented world organization in a matter of months. The
delegates and ordinary people everywhere were strongly motivated for change by the unspeakable horrors of the recent
world war. In addition, well-timed and far-sighted leadership
was provided by President Roosevelt and several other world
leaders. We believe that a similar confluence of events, popular
support, and enlightened leadership will lead to the creation of
a democratic world government; but it is a tragic reality of our
planet's history that a major conflagration will probably have to
precede and motivate the creation of the government of all
humankind.

We have argued in this book that today's global citizens'
movements for peace and justice may well provide the needed

initiative for building one world democracy when the timing is right; we believe global grassroots efforts will take the lead at times by asserting and expressing the innate sovereignty of the world's people in unmistakable ways.

But the assent of elected politicians will also be crucial. In theory, even without the participation of a popular movement, a world-wide emergency or catastrophe could motivate a critical mass of the heads of state of countries to agree to a global union. This could give us a world government overnight—at least a potentially dangerous top-down version. We allude to this possibility to prove the point that those who now exercise state power are *de facto* in an immediate position to delegate their war-making powers or other powers to a minimalist world government.

Here's a more hopeful scenario: If several prestigious major powers seized the day—as a preventive measure—and proposed a draft of a democratic world constitution open to all states to discuss and ratify, we might soon see the evolution of a global government. In such a situation, we envision that grassroots movements of global citizens would rise to the occasion in concert with such an initiative from the top. They would insist that their respective nations sign on to the movement, while pressuring delegates to incorporate the highest of democratic and human rights traditions into the provisions of the new constitution.

Nor is it far-fetched to imagine that a visionary politician of the stature of a Wilson or a Roosevelt, under the pressure of world events, could arise in the US and call for a constitutional convention to replace the UN Charter. With this sort of leadership from the world's greatest power, a world convention might easily happen. Once a constitution convention was convened, global citizens' groups and NGOs would no doubt be integral to the process of designing a global legislature. Earlier we considered a related scenario, in which an advisory world legislature becomes the "political cover" for visionary politicians who would base their call for change on its de facto legitimacy.

Any of the scenarios listed above could occur inside or outside the framework of the United Nations. Even a group of less powerful nations could initiate the process of calling a constitutional convention or forming a limited global government open to all nations—again, within or outside of the UN system. And there are many other top-down or bottom-up scenarios one could imagine. The democracies of the world could form a federation open to all democratic countries; NATO could be expanded and incorporated into the UN as a world security force; even the US under a visionary president could invite other democratic countries to federate with it under a modified US constitution.

The same objective can be achieved in many different ways; one can build a house out of different materials using different designs, but still end up with a suitable home. Of course, some materials and designs may be more efficient than others. The same is true for the work of creating global government. There are a number of possible ways to build it well, with all the previously identified key ingredients getting incorporated in a variety of workable configurations. In this chapter we will examine a few of these scenarios.

Regional organizations could create a restructured UN

A number of important regional treaty organizations already exist today, including the Organization of the American States, the African Union, the EU, NATO, the

Association of Southeast Asian Nations, and the Arab League. Some of these, such as the European Union and to a lesser extent the African Union, are evolving toward becoming genuine federations of states. As international law develops in each part of the world in accord with regional standards and traditions, such regional groups could become stepping stones toward a governed world. There is in fact nothing that can prevent regional governments from becoming a legitimate level of government above local, state, provincial, and national levels, but just below the global level that is now emerging. Thus, one future possibility is a global government set up by means of regional government representation, with each continent or regional government being seated in a world legislature and in a world executive body.

One obvious way to start such a process would be by restructuring the UN Security Council. The first step would be to abolish the veto of the so-called permanent members (Britain, China, France, Russia and the United States) that has rendered the UN so ineffective in the past. The veto would be replaced with the majority rule of the members of the Security Council themselves. The second step would be to expand the Security Council to include non-represented regions, thus making it into a representative microcosm of the world's major powers and regions. Britain and France, for example, would be represented under the EU, Arab states by the Arab League, African countries by the African Union, and Latin American countries by the Organization of the American States. In the end, all nations would be represented either by themselves, if they are large enough, or by a regional organization if they are small. This would allow China, the US, and Russia to remain on the Security Council but would give proportional representation to the rest of the world. In one fell swoop, such reforms by the UN would help it gain respect as a truly global organization, as opposed to one that merely represents the developed countries. (It should be noted that the Council now includes ten rotating, non-permanent members who lack veto power. At the time of this writing the UN is considering a proposal to add six new permanent seats without veto power that would be allotted to two nations from Asia, two from Africa, one from Europe and one from the Americas.)

The technique of combining smaller countries into regions that have true representation on the Security Council would in turn encourage the development of regional supra-national governments with many secondary benefits accruing to these regions. This step of redesigning the Security Council might then set the stage for further changes to the structure of the UN that would lead to a new global constitution and the eventual adoption of measures equivalent to enforceable global law.

A union of democracies is a logical place to start

It would seem only right that member nations of a democratic world government would themselves be democracies. It's a matter of common sense: If member nations are democratic and free of corruption, a federation of these nations will also be democratic and free of corruption. There is a direct correlation between peace, justice, the rule of law, and freely elected self-rule.

Thus, one viable way to move toward a governed world may well be that a group of democracies chooses to create a federation that is open to any country that meets minimal standards, much in the same way that the European Union has extended its federation to new countries in its region that agree to the EU's human rights standards. The practical basis of this approach is that nations who share an explicit commitment to a common set of democratic values should find it easier to form a common supranational government.

The nations of today's world are obviously at various stages of political development, but most seem to be converging on a democratic standard of government; in fact, we've noted that the majority are now democracies. Of course, others remain mired in dictatorship or monarchy. Proponents of a "union of democracies" such as the Association to Unite the Democracies (AUD) make a logical case that we need not wait until all nations are democratic before we launch a constitutional global government—we already have a critical mass of democratic nations that could form the kernel of a world union. These member nations would gain entrance to the union if, for example, they can reliably demonstrate that they hold free elections. The democratization of the planet needs to be encouraged by enlightened progressives and the free peoples of the world. A global union of democracies that sets standards and provides assistance to non-members would greatly accelerate this process.

A worldwide constitutional convention is a plausible vehicle

Another approach to creating a governed world would be to convene a world constitutional convention, as was once attempted in the 1950s and 1960s by the World Constitution and Parliament Association. A powerful joint call from respected world leaders might be enough to launch the unprecedented work of creating a global constitution to replace the UN Charter. Like the union of democracies discussed above, this variant would be rather bold in that it would operate fully outside of the UN framework.

The call would specify that a constitutional convention should be convened in some world capital, such as Paris, Cairo, Beijing, Geneva, or New York, or rotate between them. At this grand meeting, the details of a proposed constitution would be hammered out by delegates or ambassadors sent from willing nations, regional groups, or representatives of an advisory world parliament—as outlined in chapter four. Delegates or advisors might even come from certain NGOs, from the world's religions, from professional associations, or from other civil society groups.

In response to the call, one could imagine that the world's greatest jurists, lawyers, politicians, and visionary social thinkers would convene with high fanfare. A great and historic debate would then begin. This would be similar to how the delegates to the American Constitutional Convention worked out the details of the American federal constitution through a series of compromises. Citizens' groups of all kinds and the world's media would no doubt offer input and be in observance during the process; their assertions of world public opinion would weigh heavily in the deliberations.

Such a new world constitution would be years or even a decade or two in the making. But once ratified by a critical mass of nations, it would one day become the founding document of a new democratic world order—and that date would forever be celebrated as "Constitution Day" for the planet!

A major problem to be faced by the world constitutional convention will be the system of representation, an issue we have broached earlier. Delegates from large countries would justly fear that small countries might obtain too large a voice as they do today in the General Assembly; but the delegates from small countries might protest that their voices will be drowned out by a myriad of representatives from the larger powers in a system based on population. The Founding Fathers of the United States solved this dilemma with the so-called Great Compromise that led to our bicameral Congress (i.e., the Senate with two members from each state regardless of size, and the House whose representation is based on population in each state). The delegates to the world constitutional assembly would have to struggle to find a similar compromise. They would need to scrutinize the many voting models that have been proposed (such as Richard Hudson's Binding Triad[1]), or proposed global constitutions already in existence, and then creatively draft a fair system of power sharing based on a variety of factors, such as population and economic contribution.

Instituting checks and balances among different branches of the world government would, of course, be a central concern of the delegates to a world constitutional convention. These deliberations will prevent too much power from being concentrated in one branch or person. Libertarian thinkers and human rights activists will no doubt be on hand to ensure that the constitutional convention includes powerful safeguards against the danger of tyranny.

The framers of a new world constitution must also invent a new system of justice to promote enforceable global law. This system would build on existing treaty law, as well as the statues of the ICC and the International Court of Justice, but also go far beyond current international law by creating a body of law that would apply *uniformly to all world citizens of the member-states.*

For this global enforcement system to work against rogue

states, surviving terrorist groups, or organized crime, the constitutional convention will need to debate the provisions governing a standing world military force. The constitution will have to give this force enough strength to settle large disputes, but not be so powerful as to create a potential threat to peace itself. If the world executive branch decided to enforce a decision of a world court or uphold an existing law, it would be the job of this world military force to back up the world marshals who would have the frontline duty of law enforcement. This may seem a daunting prospect, but compare this scenario with our current war system that includes nearly a trillion dollars per year spent worldwide to maintain the readiness of over a hundred national armies. This system of ritualized insanity would be replaced by a few hundred thousand "world policeman" and global soldiers who would preserve planetary law and order at a fraction of the cost.

Once the joint document is completed, nations would agree to a world government constitution and ratify it by voting for accession, similar to the way nations now join the European Union. They would then legally and formally transfer designated parts of their sovereign power upward, beginning with their "right" to make war. They would also agree to be bound by the decisions of world courts in dispute resolution.

It will take a great deal of effort and risk to achieve adherence to world law by all states, but the potential rewards are tremendous. For example, the first priority of a global government would be total elimination of nuclear weapons. It would achieve this goal worldwide in an organized manner by using the full power of law; the destruction of weapons would be verified by global inspectors.

The second priority would be the elimination of conventional war. This could be accomplished with binding dispute resolution, regulated disarmament, and a superior international UN security force for emergency situations. Nations would transfer both their right to make war and control of their national armies to the world legislature, which would then be the only body allowed to use military force across national borders. In the beginning of the development of global government, the federation might need to use force against non-member nations that engage in aggressive behavior. Nations that refused to join a global government could be persuaded to join by economic incentives and the protection provided by the rule of law.

Once all states have joined the federation, the need for military operations would become minimal. The world legislature or the world courts would be in a position to authorize any use of force required for the purpose of implementing a peace settlement or enforcing a court ruling.

A system based on world law will give everyone greater security than do the entire world's costly armies, navies, and air forces combined. Removing the burden of maintaining a military will provide tremendous economic benefits to every nation. For example, in 1948, following a civil war, Costa Rica announced that it no longer needed an army and it disbanded its military. Since then, the country has relied on the Organization of the American States and the Rio Treaty to protect it from invasion. Costa Rica has maintained its independence despite its location between two rather turbulent neighbors: Nicaragua and Panama. Costa Rica has the highest standard of living and one of the least corrupt governments of Latin America.

The two other examples of countries that were freed

from the burden of militarism are Japan and Germany. After their defeat in World War II, they wrote into their constitutions severe limits on military development and involvement. The Japanese constitution of 1947 went so far as to state that Japan "forever renounces war as a sovereign right of a nation and the threat or use of force as a means of settling international disputes." Both countries are now among the most prosperous in the world.

Just imagine what the world could do if it were at peace. Nations could focus on free trade and consequently create a stronger global economy. Scientists could effectively address issues of population control, disease, and environmental damage. Governments could redirect precious resources from defense to ending world hunger. With so much of our precious time, energy, money, and intelligence no longer being wasted on war, we could create a much better world for ourselves and our descendants.

As more nations join the federation, the massive armaments the world now has will simply become obsolete. Of course, nations would retain an internal military force similar to the US National Guard to be used for disasters or civil unrest. A global federal government would have a common external policy to deal with nations outside of the federation, just as each state in America shares the one foreign policy set by the US federal government.

If the major nations of the world that control most of the military power joined a global government at its founding, then smaller, less powerful nations would soon follow. Failed states engaged in nation-building with the help of the new world community would automatically be inducted into the world federation. A stable nation could, in theory, exist outside of the union as long as it did not violate global law.

Eventually, all nations of the world would join of their own free will due to the numerous advantages of membership. They would quickly see how they would be protected from foreign invasion and terrorism by the power of the law backed by global government; they would be relieved of the burden of large military budgets; and they would gain the economic advantages of free trade and fewer restrictions within the governed area. These benefits would be similar to what a state in the US currently enjoys as part of the American federal union. Individuals within such a system would feel more secure and would enjoy greater freedom to travel and a wider range of economic options just as members of the European Union now experience.

This approach to building a global government will take time and years of debate and struggle. Nations may be reluctant to join and give up control over their military to an untried organization.

Wars in today's world are most frequently civil wars rather than violations of a border by one nation against another. Because the parties are not always nations, it is important that rebel groups have their cases heard in a world court. A court that has the power to settle disputes could end many of the world's current ongoing civil wars, such as the devastating conflicts now scarring Congo and Sudan in Africa.

The transition to effective global government based on a new constitution will require leadership and statesmanship on a level not previously experienced. It will not be an easy task to bring the world under the constitutional rule of law, but the option of remaining insecure under the anarchic war system is unacceptable.

The EU offers a historic model of a union of nations

The creation of a global government may well be accomplished by expanding the European Union. This surprising idea makes sense for several reasons. Chief among these is that the EU is already accomplished in doing exactly what a global government would need to do: convincing nations to give up some of their sovereignty for the sake of something better.

With the evolution of the EU out of the ashes of WWII, Europe has, once again, shown us the way of the future. After inventing democracy in Athens 2,500 years ago, after giving us the Magna Charta and the system of national sovereignty created by the Peace of Westphalia in 1648, after evolving the ideals of liberalism and humanism that culminated in the French and American revolutions, it has now created the supranational constitution. What has happened in Europe is not just a bureaucratic reshuffling; it is a revolution in human affairs.

From the beginning, the EU was envisioned by such leaders as Winston Churchill to be Europe's best method for preventing future wars in Europe. A French statesman named Jean Monnet, who is often referred to as "the father of Europe," was responsible for much of the original design and is credited with holding the vision. The EU has grown into a genuine political union of states with a directly elected parliament located in Brussels, Belgium and Strasbourg, France. Its budget of 100 billion dollars is generated from sales tax, and most of the Union now has a common currency: the euro.

Once a country joins the EU, its citizens are citizens of the Union and have the right to live and work in any of its member-countries, just as US citizens can live and work in any US state.

The EU moved in the 1990s from a complex system of treaties and law to a real constitutional government of Europe. The EU constitution's official motto is "Unity in Diversity." As we have noted, the EU constitution sets standards for membership, both economically and politically; for instance, it does not admit countries that support the death penalty.

One country after another has voted for accession to the union. The willingness to receive the benefits of supranational law has provided the key motivation. In May 2004, ten countries, mostly former Soviet bloc nations, became full members of the EU: Cyprus, the Czech Republic, Estonia, Latvia, Lithuania, Hungary, Malta, Poland, Slovenia, and Slovakia, bringing the total membership to twenty-five. The EU had fifteen member-countries before the expansion. They were Austria, Belgium, Denmark, Finland, France, Germany, Greece, Ireland, Italy, Luxembourg, the Netherlands, Portugal, Spain, Sweden, and the United Kingdom. The population of the EU is now 450 million, making it the third largest sovereign area after China and India.

It is not inconceivable that Russia and the other former Soviet republics may join as well. Turkey has applied for membership, which lends hope of expanding the Union into Muslim countries. Other countries that have strong ties to Europe, such as Australia, Canada, and Israel, may be candidates in the future.

With the addition of its new Eastern European members, the EU's gross national product is now seven trillion dollars, close to that of the US.[1] The EU is also developing a rapid-response joint military force that requires member nations to contribute toward maintaining a standing army of 50,000 to 60,000 troops that can be deployed for up to a year to deal with military threats around the world.[2] But this is a small force compared to the US military; the EU, in general, has not militarized.

This new reign of international peace in Europe was achieved not at the end of the barrel of a gun, but through diplomacy and mutually agreed upon laws. Conflicts between old adversaries, such as France and Germany, which fought two world wars against each other, seem to have finally been put to rest. No one today even remotely thinks that France and Germany could fight one another again.

The peace achieved in Europe through the EU's experiment with supranational law is an outstanding model for world peace. The establishment of a united Europe and the attainment of peace between old adversaries set an example for the entire world. These achievements show the value of supranational law, cooperation, and diplomacy.

With regard to foreign policy, the EU does not yet speak with one voice. Each country is still free to set its own foreign policy. The constitution is not yet strong enough for a single foreign policy, as evidenced by the sharp split of opinion over joining the US invasion of Iraq in 2003. The EU also does not yet have a common currency in all member countries. The EU is not yet fully a true federation, but significant power is shifting to the central government. It has followed the rallying call of "ever closer union" for years. The EU is in the process of evolving from a confederation to a federation.

As it expands, the EU will act as a force to support and reform the UN and, as noted earlier, the EU may move toward being a single voice in the UN. This would be done by consolidating the votes of the member-countries to one vote in the Security Council and by transferring the vetoes of Britain and France to the EU block. A common defense policy for the EU is developing and will need to be coordinated with NATO.

Some believe that expanding the European Union by opening it up to non-European countries would be a viable way to create a world government and would perhaps be easier than reforming the UN. The EU does not have the problem of veto power, and it maintains high standards for membership. The EU has been dynamic and evolving in its structure, unlike the UN, which has seen little reform to its Charter.

On the other hand, there is a major downside to going this route. It would most likely be many years before the majority of the nations of the world would join. This leaves open the risk that before the union is truly global, it would be challenged by another large, sovereign power, possibly leading to violent conflict.

On the other hand, a constitutional convention for creating a totally new global organization poses the same problem. Such a body could be started by as few as two countries willing to draft and ratify a constitution that would be open to all countries to join. After all, the EU began with only two countries that were buying steel and coal together, so anything is possible. A small group of brave countries could start a global federation without having to overcome all the obstacles they would encounter if they tried to do it through the UN, most notably the issue of the big power veto. But growth would likely be very slow, and the world's problems need urgent attention.

Given this reality, we believe that the best method of creating global government would probably be the remaking of the UN through a historic constitutional convention called from within the UN to reform its Charter. This would automatically involve most of the nations of the world and would avoid splitting the world into two or three sovereign units that could fall into a war. Radical UN reform is the most efficient path because the existing machinery of the UN could itself be utilized in the transformation; otherwise a new organization must be created from the ground up—a slow and difficult process indeed. But can all this really be done in a reasonable amount of time?

Restructuring the United Nations is feasible and desirable

In 1945, the UN was established with the hope of eliminating the scourge of war. Tragically, it was created without the power to accomplish that objective. The UN is not a government and can neither make nor enforce world law. The reason for its general lack of success at peacemaking lies in the fact that it has no leverage to control warring parties and no enforcement mechanism if nations or factions do not live up to their commitments.

Sixty years later, the UN urgently needs radical reform. The world is teeming with rogue states, terrorists, and other aggrieved parties who lack access to justice through enforceable global law—but *do* have access to weapons of mass destruction. Obviously, there are many other dire global issues that also must be addressed by a restructured UN. Convening a world constitutional convention to revise the UN Charter is a feasible and worthy long-term goal for any world-citizen activist. Barring that, certainly incremental reforms are needed now to avert disaster.

Under the original UN Charter, the Security Council was intended to be the UN's central decision-making body as well as its chief peacekeeping instrument. It can vote to condemn acts of aggression and impose sanctions, and in theory it can vote to mobilize ad hoc military interventions, using a force comprised of troops assembled from member-countries. The General Assembly, which is made up of one representative from each country, can only pass resolutions that are essentially recommendations.

As we have noted, the Security Council is now made up of fifteen countries: the five permanent members who possess veto power, and ten other countries who rotate in every two years. The veto power of the permanent members—the United States, the United Kingdom, France, Russia, and China—provide the chief illustration of why the UN has become virtually obsolete in our dangerous times. Simply by virtue of being the victors of a war six decades past (and in the case of Russia and China, the successors of these victors), these five countries can, without appeal, block any resolution passed by the General Assembly or the Security Council. This tyrannical right of veto is an affront to the sovereignty of the people of the world and the democratic rights of world citizens, not to mention an insult to the rights of other member-nations of the UN. Today there are other great powers of roughly equal weight in the world in comparison to the permanent members of the Security Council, including India, Brazil, Germany, Italy, Spain, Indonesia, Korea, and Japan.

The ongoing dispute between Israel and the Palestinians provides perhaps the most egregious example of the debilitating power of the veto. For decades, and in overwhelming numbers, both the Security Council and the General Assembly have passed resolutions calling on Israel to withdraw from the occupied territories. All of these sincere initiatives for justice have been blocked by the US veto, thus contributing to the shameful inability of the UN to resolve this protracted dispute that threatens world peace.

Thus far, the UN has used sanctions and limited military intervention to try to enforce the resolutions of the Security Council that pass without veto. UN sanctions are a very blunt instrument; all too often, they cause egregious suffering for the people of the target nation without directly impacting the offending government. Such was obviously the case when the UN instituted sanctions against Iraq. The military interventions of the UN have also been failures, by and large. The genocide in Rwanda in 1994, in which the UN and the international community completely failed to respond to the massacre of some 800,000 people, marks one of the lowest points in the UN's sad record of military diplomacy; one only need watch the film *Hotel Rwanda* to get a taste of the worst consequences of today's anarchic international system and the UN's impotence in the face of it. At the time of this writing, we are witnessing yet another rendition of African genocide, and yet another example of the UN's inability to save lives, in the Darfour region of Sudan. When will the world's people be willing to say that enough is enough?

What can we say on the positive side? The UN does play a role as a facilitator of communication among all nations. It provides a place where hostile countries can meet on neutral ground. Since its inception, the UN has mediated a number of minor disputes with success. It was recently able to resolve the long-standing conflict between East Timor and Indonesia, establishing East Timor as an independent state and member of the UN. However, the UN was powerless to prevent the original catastrophe in East Timor: After the illegal invasion and annexation of the island by Indonesia in 1975, with the covert support of the US, over 200,000 people (a third of the population) died from massacre and forced starvation.

It is a tragedy of immense proportions that most such acts of aggression since the UN's establishment have gone unchecked and unpunished. One cause of the UN's weakness is the crippling veto; another is its lack of a standing army that can move quickly enough to prevent conflicts in the first place. The UN's so-called peacekeeping forces are normally called in to maintain the peace (or conditions of truce) once a military conflict has ended. But the weakness of UN peacekeeping was amply demonstrated by the events in 1995 at Srebrenica, Bosnia, where 400 lightly armed Dutch peacekeepers stood by as more than 7,000 Muslim men and boys were massacred after being forcefully removed from a UN "safe area."[3] This was the trigger for NATO's intervention, led by the US. A restructured UN will create a standing rapid-response force not dominated by any one nation or coalition, as was this NATO intervention and the first Gulf War in 1991.

The UN has also been a force for progress in international law, creating more than 35,000 treaties and related pieces of international law and over 500 multinational treaties.[4] Perhaps its best achievement in the area of security, as we have seen, has been the creation of the International Criminal Court (ICC), which investigates and tries individuals accused of genocide, war crimes, and crimes against humanity.

The ICC offers a more expedient way—in a world of anarchy—to deal with the most flagrant violations of "international law"; before its development, special ad hoc tribunals had to be established on a case-by-case basis. The development of the ICC is a positive step toward the development of supranational law and toward global government. But it is far from offering a genuine system of justice that can consistently deliver and enforce binding decisions with each violation of law. The ICC offers an incremental improvement, but its American critics are not incorrect when they insist that this new court is easily politicized and could evolve in dangerous directions. We've already noted that the ICC lacks oversight from a world legislature and is not backed by the legitimacy of a constitutional world government that provides checks and balances on abuses of power.

For these and many other reasons that include the threat of global warming, there can be little doubt that radical restructuring of the UN may be the most important item on the world's agenda today—along with a grassroots movement for a global peoples' legislature. UN Secretary General Kofi Annan himself called for "radical reform" of the UN in 2003. He made this urgent call after the terrible bombing of the UN headquarters in Baghdad, where the UN had come to be seen as a mere extension of an aggressive US policy. It is a bitter irony that Secretary Annan found himself later admitting on BBC Radio that he considered the US invasion of Iraq to be "illegal" and a "violation of the UN Charter."

Below we recommend three fundamental reforms that we believe are feasible in the short run. Obviously, it remains to be seen what genuine reforms may actually grow out of the UN's credibility crisis, and who will lead the charge at this critical juncture.

A few critical reforms could transform the UN

Part and parcel of the UN's credibility problem is its lack of basic standards for membership. Even the worst military dictatorships can be members, and are members; disturbingly,

such oppressive governments are even admitted to membership on the UN Human Rights Commission. No country has
ever been expelled from the UN, even for the most heinous
crimes of aggression. Highly undemocratic and even criminal
regimes have an equal vote in the UN General Assembly along
with every other member. Additionally, powerful nations
like the US are able to manipulate the UN for their own
advantage.

The first step in radically reforming the UN should be to
require that all its voting members are countries that hold free
elections and are not acting in violation of international law.
Limiting the initial voting membership of the reformed organization to such governments has two benefits. First, the votes
they cast will have a better chance of being representative of
the will of the world community as opposed to the self-interest of a dictatorship or isolated oligarchy. Second, dictatorships
and absolute monarchies will feel pressure to democratize in
order to regain their influence in the UN and a position of
prestige in world affairs. Economic incentives as well as elec-
tion-monitoring assistance could help bring these countries
closer to established democratic standards and eventual voting
membership.

The second big step in reforming the UN is to give it the
power to enforce its decisions fairly, uniformly, and swiftly.
At a minimum, this new power would enable a restructured
UN to intervene anywhere in the world to *prevent* civil wars
and international conflicts from getting out of control. For
example, the civil war in the Congo has taken over one million
lives in the last four years, with little intervention by the UN
or international community. Only the binding power of
enforceable global law can be effective in regions that lack
strategic significance; experience shows that most countries are

not motivated enough to intervene in such remote conflicts for strictly humanitarian reasons.

Sadly, where national sovereignty reigns supreme, national self-interest is usually the basis of any response to an international crisis. Under our current system in which self-interest is the highest level of concern, the moral obligation to alleviate human suffering ends at the border. Under a true system of global law, the world would respond immediately to any act of aggression—even in remote corners of the world. That's because law by its nature must be enforced uniformly all across the sovereign area, and because fundamental human rights are at stake. As a beginning incremental step toward this posture, a standing rapid-response force must be made available through the UN to intervene in such crises. Its military burden should be shared equally and financial costs evenly distributed.

The third step in reforming the UN is to make the body at least nominally democratic. As we have noted, the veto power must be removed. In addition, the UN needs a new system of voting. If democracy is to be expanded to the global level, voting power must be based at least in part on the number of people represented. Under the current UN system in the General Assembly, each country has one vote. That means that India, with over a billion people, has the same voting power as Iceland, with just over a quarter of a million people. Many practical proposals for weighted voting are currently on the table of policymakers. Political pressure from a provisional or advisory world legislature could also mightily move this type of reform along.

The fourth critical reform is the establishment of a UN tax base that drastically increases the budget of the UN. The UN needs a system of mandatory taxes that can provide a steady stream of income that is not subject to tampering by countries with political agendas. The current budget of eleven billion dollars per year is a pittance compared to a world military budget approaching one trillion dollars per year.

Can the UN be reformed to become a real supranational government—or is a totally new organization needed? It is possible to reform the UN, but it will not be easy. The UN Charter states that amending the charter requires a two-thirds majority of the General Assembly and the approval of all five permanent Security Council members. That is a tough but not insurmountable obstacle. The charter was amended in 1965 to increase the number of countries on the Security Council from eleven to fifteen. The countries with veto power will give up their control only when they are put under pressure from the rest of the world and when they become aware of the advantages in doing so.

There are great benefits to using the groundwork that has been laid by the UN to create a democratic world-governing body. First, it has respect as the most recognizable international institution. Second, the vast logistical challenge of going around it to form another organization seems less likely to succeed.

There have been many calls down through the years for UN reform by member-countries and NGOs, but few have gone so far as to ask for the reforms that have just been described—a democratic overhaul of the organization with changes to the power structure and the establishment of a tax base and a standing army.

We believe that the quickest, least risky, and most legitimate path to this overhaul would be for a group of nations to call for a constitutional convention of all UN members, for citizens' groups to support this call with a worldwide campaign of education and agitation, and through the organization of an ad hoc world peoples' assembly or world legislature. This method would be much faster than, for example, adding one or two members at a time to a regional government such as the EU, or starting over from scratch with a convention outside the UN—and speedy reform is now essential. The UN route would be less risky because it would include the overwhelming majority of nations right from the start.

An opportunity like no other stands before us

Some may proclaim that the world is not ready for the drastic changes discussed in this chapter; they will assert that any such transformation is unlikely to occur anytime soon. To them we reply that the world has never been more ready and that global government is our only option if we are to avoid catastrophe.

The UN Charter was signed six weeks before Hiroshima was destroyed by a nuclear explosion. Had the UN been created *after* the first use of atomic weapons, its structure might have been different; most likely nuclear weapons would have been put under international control, as was almost accomplished by the famous Baruch Plan in 1946. We cannot change history, but we can make our generation's contribution to history by, at a minimum, placing nuclear weapons under international control.

There is a continual upward evolution of the moral fabric of society. No longer do we find infanticide, cannibalism, or slavery to be morally acceptable. These practices have been outlawed in every nation of the world. The next step in this moral evolution of humankind is the abolition of war.

Let us not be slaves to our savage past. War is morally wrong; war is the greatest of all evils; now a viable alternative to war exists. And now an effective alternative to global environmental destruction exists.

The opportunity now before us is unique to our generation. The abolition of war is now within our grasp. We must demand the most basic human right of all, the right to exist and to be free of the threat of war. We must enlarge our idea of patriotism to include our duty to the planet and humanity, not just our country.

*I pledge allegiance to the Earth, and to the
planet for which it stands; one world, under law,
indivisible, with liberty and justice for all.*
—Martin Hayes

Part II

Global Problems that Need Global Solutions

7

Eliminating Nuclear Weapons

Since Auschwitz we know what man is capable of.
And since Hiroshima we know what is at stake.
—Victor Frankl

Hiroshima changed our world forever. The advent of "the bomb" was yet another horror to compound the devastation left behind by the war in Europe. As the revulsion over Hiroshima and Nagasaki spread, a desperate sense arose in many quarters that mankind was facing certain doom unless nuclear weapons technology was brought under the control of a world government.

"One world or none!" suddenly became the oft-repeated slogan of laymen, intellectuals, and even atomic scientists. Albert Einstein joined a chorus of prominent leaders and intellectuals who argued for the urgent necessity of a supranational government with greater powers than the newly formed United Nations. "Mankind's desire for peace," wrote Einstein in 1946, "can be realized only by the creation of a world government."[1] Einstein's words seem even more prophetic today, as human kind has failed so far to contain the spread of the bomb and other weapons of mass destruction (WMDs).

A fatal turning point occurred in the latter half of 1946. In a unilateral gesture almost unthinkable today, the US made an offer at the United Nations to surrender its death weapon to an international authority, detailed in what became known as the Baruch Plan. The plan had features of enforceable global law, and was widely supported by advocates of world government. The defeat of this initiative by December 1946 provides a key lesson for today's world democracy activists: The world federalist movement remained divided into bickering factions throughout 1946, unable to unite around this historic prop-osal. The Baruch Plan died an early death, and by 1947 a nuclear arms race had descended upon the world.

Since then, the prospect of nuclear war has hovered over the planet like a sword of Damocles. The convergence of the bomb with a "war system" based on the delusion of unlimited national sovereignty remains the gravest threat facing humankind. The control and eventual abolition of nuclear weapons and WMDs will be the highest priority task of the coming democratic world government.

Controlling "nukes" will require peoples' power

Nuclear war is not an option in any scenario. Those who endured the years of President Ronald Reagan's build-up toward a nuclear confrontation with the Soviet Union in the mid-1980s will remember the scary descriptions of "nuclear winter." In the aftermath of a full nuclear exchange, the amount of debris blown into the atmosphere would block the rays of the sun for several years, creating a drastic lowering of the earth's temperature and triggering mass extinctions. Even without a nuclear winter, the amount of radiation released would kill most of the human population on earth and alter the world's environment forever.

Proving Einstein right, the United Nations has been impotent in the face of accelerating nuclear proliferation;

.   the veto power in the Security Council rendered the UN superfluous while the US and the Soviet Union stockpiled thousands of nuclear warheads and other WMDs, and as nuclear weapons soon spread to the UK, France, and China, and then Israel, India, and Pakistan.

After the fall of the Berlin Wall in 1989, one might have hoped for a more significant reduction in nuclear stockpiles— some sort of peace dividend. But the US has neither disarmed fully nor closed its nuclear installations around the world. The insanity of the nuclear threat continues: The US and Russia still have enough nuclear firepower to threaten the existence of all people on earth. And the economies and political culture of America and Russia are still in recovery from decades of living on the brink of nuclear suicide.

Much as the visionary Baruch Plan got scuttled long ago, the US has squandered the historic opportunities created by the end of the Cold War and the introduction of a market economy in China. With the help of the other nuclear powers, it might have moved swiftly in the wake of the fall of communism to create a post-nuclear age based on enforceable global law. This would have been the ideal. Instead, it appears that the task of creating a world without nuclear weapons, not to mention the abolition of conventional war, must come from a progressive worldwide movement of people that will eventually lead to the creation of a federal world government. Sixty years after Hiroshima, our leaders have failed to rise to Einstein's call.

We must face the challenge of nuclear proliferation

Even after the reductions of the last decade or so, the US still has approximately 7,500 nuclear weapons. Of these,

2,000 to 2,500 remain on hair-trigger alert, ready to launch at a moment's notice. The US has a fleet of submarines bearing nuclear weapons ready to launch that are only fifteen minutes away from most targets. As if this were not enough, we also have 1,750 nuclear weapons on intercontinental planes that are ready to launch.[2]

Russia keeps between 2,000 and 2,500 nuclear weapons on hair-trigger alert as well. It has approximately 9,000 nuclear weapons in its entire arsenal.

But we are far from the simpler days of a balance of terror between the US and Russia; the asymmetric spread of nuclear weapons to countries in a variety of regions of the world has greatly increased the chances of their use. Today China has approximately 400 nuclear weapons; France, 350; the United Kingdom, 185; Israel, 200; India 60, and Pakistan somewhere between 24 and 48. North Korea has a few nuclear weapons but it is unknown exactly how many.[3] Iran also has a nuclear program that the West and the UN are attempting to control.

As smaller countries have gained nuclear weapons technology, the world has become all the more dangerous. This threat of proliferation was foreshadowed during the 1973 Yom Kippur War, as Israel put the nuclear option on the table when its defeat looked possible. A chilling recent example is that of Pakistan and India, now both nuclear powers, who alarmed the world in May 2002 when they raised the possibility of a nuclear exchange because of an unresolved dispute over Kashmir. Also disturbing was the revelation early in 2005 that Pakistan had sacked its top nuclear scientist amid a probe into the secret sale of nuclear technology to Iran and Libya. This scientist, A.Q. Kahn, is known as the "father" of the Islamic world's atomic bomb.

Pakistan has yet to agree to a "no-first-use" policy—meaning it could respond to a conventional threat with a nuclear response. Pakistan is home to a large Muslim fundamentalist population and is currently governed by an unpopular military dictator who has survived several assassination attempts. Control of this country's nuclear weapons could easily fall into the hands of fundamentalist Muslim leaders and their fanatical followers in the event of a coup or revolution.

Terrorist organizations including al Qaeda have made numerous documented attempts to buy nuclear weapons on the black market. We've noted that experts widely believe that the chances of a terrorist group acquiring and using nuclear weapons are high. Islamic terrorists would lack the restraint of a nation; they would not be deterred by the threat of retaliation because there would be no specific nation or locale against which to retaliate. In the final analysis, the only way this threat can be contained is through a worldwide ban on nuclear weapons and other WMDs, backed by the security and justice that only a system of enforceable world law can provide.

No nation has a "right" to possess nuclear weapons

Most people block out the frightening reality of living in a nuclear age; we all have a shared numbness to the facts about the potential of nuclear destruction. Because nuclear weapons were used only twice at the end of World War II, many people seem to assume that the bomb will never be used again.

To be fair, we must acknowledge that some progress has been made. As of 2005, the number of nukes is half what it was at the peak of the Cold War. The US and Russia have agreed to another round of weapons reductions that will cut their collective nuclear stockpile by two-thirds by 2010. The states that once comprised the Soviet Union have chosen not to be nuclear powers and have transferred their nuclear weapons to Russia or destroyed them. South Africa had nuclear weapons before apartheid ended but fortunately chose to give them up under the leadership of Nelson Mandela.

But this progress may be too little too late. Neither the US nor any other country can stop continued nuclear proliferation if a state or a terrorist group is determined to join the nuclear club. Nuclear weapons the size of a suitcase can be delivered anywhere in the world, and many are thought to have disappeared from Russia. How can one defend against this sort of proliferation? The folly of building a supposed nuclear shield in space—the ongoing legacy of the so-called "Star Wars" space defense—represents a dangerous and tragic way of avoiding America's true responsibilities to the planet. The war on terrorism may fatten the budgets of the military-industrial-intelligence complex in Washington, but it cannot guarantee that a nuke will never be smuggled into the US. The only hope for a "defense" against nuclear terror is the technique that has worked throughout history: social justice and equity obtained through law and democratic government.

In addition, one might well ask: What gives one nation the right to have nuclear weapons, but not some other nation? What nation or group possesses the right to decide who belongs to the nuclear club, and who does not? One of the largest obstacles to controlling nuclear proliferation is the hypocrisy at the heart of global nuclear policy. Those world powers that today are pressuring countries like Iran and North Korea to forsake the nuclear option are themselves clinging to the bomb as the centerpiece of their own security. This makes it rather strange for these countries to claim that it is morally reprehensible for others to possess nuclear weapons, but still morally acceptable for themselves to rely on them!

Of course, our answer is that *no nation should have the right to possess nuclear weapons;* they are simply too dangerous and should be banned by world law. Getting nations to destroy their nuclear weapons will require a set of rules that apply equally to all countries and are enforced by a neutral world body. Under the current war system, each nation strives to protect itself and thus tries to acquire the most advanced weapons available. Therefore, it will require replacing the "protection" provided by those weapons with the protection of a global security system controlled by a democratic world government. Nuclear-overkill arsenals like those of the US and Russia can be reduced prior to global government, but stopping proliferation and completely eliminating nuclear weapons will require global government. Only the rule of law can put an end to this scourge.

There is no way to control what sovereign states do to provide for their own security amidst global anarchy; treaties and visionary pronouncements have never worked. Only the rule of law worldwide can bring reason to a world gone mad with militarism. As we have seen, global government can settle disputes between nations in a world court that operates according to a global constitution and that safeguards the rights of individuals and nations. Only this sort of process can make the need for nuclear weapons obsolete. It is clear that we need to move forward with creating a sovereign global democracy—and that we need to do so quickly.

The next great advance in the evolution of civilization
cannot take place until war is abolished.
—Douglas MacArthur

8

Global
Sustainability
through Global Law

*Only within the moment of time represented by
the present century has one species, man, acquired
significant power to alter the nature of his world.*
—Rachel Carson

As the world has gotten smaller, its problems have
become larger—and global in scope. Many social, economic,
and environmental ills cannot be solved within individual
nations, especially in this era of economic globalization. An
economic downturn in the United States causes people to lose
their jobs in Bogota, or Hong Kong, or Athens. Environmental
damage and overpopulation in the developing world leads to
millions of illegal immigrants hopping borders to wealthier
countries. The over-consumption of fossil fuels in the developed world and the clear-cutting of forests in the developing
world is causing global warming, which in turn is affecting
agriculture by destabilizing weather conditions worldwide.

When immigrants and refugees start pouring across borders, it is the international community that is best equipped to
solve the underlying problems that are causing the migrations.
Polluted seas and rising ocean levels due to glacial melting are
every nation's concern. Global warming equally affects all
living things on this planet. In an interconnected and

interdependent world, all nations and all people are affected more than ever by the actions of their neighbors around the globe. The isolated nation-state and impotent organizations like the UN are no longer able to cope with such global problems; only democratic global government can.

The population crisis is accelerating

One of the world's most pressing problems is the daunting fact that human population growth is out of control, virtually guaranteeing us a future with more crowding and continued destruction of natural resources. While it is true that women in both developed and developing countries bear fewer children than ever before, population remains a crisis because of increased longevity; on all continents, survival rates are higher than ever before. In the last century, humankind has eliminated its natural predators, provided a relatively steady food supply, and conquered many diseases.

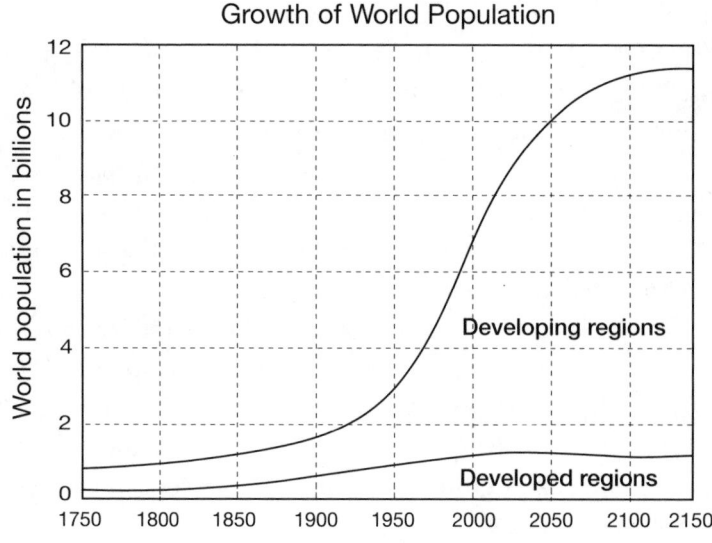

Growth of World Population

Source: UN Projections, PBS.org

Two thousand years ago, there were only about 200 million human beings on the earth. Not until the early 1800s did the population reach one billion. It doubled to two billion only 123 years later, in 1927. The third billion took only another thirty-three years; we reached it in 1960. The fourth billion took a mere thirteen years, occurring in 1974. The fifth billion was added in twelve years, in 1987. The sixth billion came twelve years later, in 1999. Today the current population is 6.3 billion and growing. The UN projects that world population will rise to between eight and ten billion in 2050.[1]

The most dramatic increase in the size of the human population has thus occurred in the last two hundred years, when it grew six-fold from one billion in the early 1800s to over six billion by 2003. Historians agree that this increase correlates directly with the rise of the Industrial Revolution and the widespread use of fossil fuels in agriculture.

The introduction of petroleum-based fertilizers and mechanized farming based on fossil fuel energy has expanded the carrying capacity of the earth. The increased quantity and quality of the food supply has allowed for a much faster rate of population growth. Modern industry—combined with the rise of scientific medicine and other arts of civilization—continues to increase longevity as well.

The inherent risk of a food supply based on petroleum should be obvious: Petroleum is a nonrenewable resource whose worldwide supply and production is peaking—according to some reliable estimates—between 2006 and 2015.[2] A declining oil supply will lead to an increase in production costs in all agricultural sectors. Increased cost of food, combined with an expanding population almost completely dependent on petroleum-based agriculture, is a formula for disaster. Unless population growth is brought under control and new sources of energy are brought online, the human species faces a precarious future.

Besides putting our own survival at risk, the human population explosion is also causing serious stress to the natural ecosystems of the world. For instance, we continue to clear forests at a catastrophic rate in order to create farmland to feed more and more people. Rainforests in particular are disappearing at a rate of one and a half acres per second; having once covered 14 percent of the planet's surface, they now cover only 6 percent. At this rate of destruction, the planet's rainforests will be gone in forty years.[3]

This process of wiping out natural ecosystems is the single most environmentally destructive act of humankind—causing, among other things, a massive wave of extinctions of plant and animal species. We lose at least one species every twenty minutes, some twenty-seven thousand species a year—a rate and scale of extinction that has not occurred since the era 65 million years ago when the dinosaurs became extinct. With the animal kingdom being destroyed at such a pace, we humans cannot be far behind.

The system that supports life on our planet is a rich but vulnerable web of life that will inevitably collapse after so many of its constituent threads are removed. The destruction of ecosystems that took millions of years to evolve cannot be restored in a generation or two; much of the environmental damage now occurring—species extinction in particular—is irreversible.

We can't go back to being hunters and gatherers, but we *can* control the population growth and land use practices that are driving environmental destruction. An important symbolic step in this direction was the awarding of the 2004 Nobel Peace Prize to Wangari Maathai, a remarkable Kenyan activist who founded a movement that empowered women to plant millions of trees in ravaged forestland all over Africa. With the formation of a global government, world parks comparable to national parks could be established in developing countries to protect land that is crucial to the entire planet's biosystem, with the expense shared by the world community. The creation of world parks and other land management practices could salvage rainforests and other ecologically sensitive areas in countries that cannot possibly plan for or manage this sort of global challenge on their own. It should be remembered that, in dealing with ecological destruction, one of the advantages of a world government is that it could factor in the needs of all nations and globally manage scarce resources on behalf of the planet as a whole.

Overpopulation has a global solution

Overpopulation is a direct cause of human misery throughout the world—especially in the developing world, where increasingly scarce resources cause people to compete daily for their basic needs. Many developing nations face a grave future of poverty and environmental destruction if their populations continue expanding at their current rate—in fact, many already do. The Malthusian theory of population growth stated that there is a reverse correlation between population and food supply. Malthus, however, missed the wild card of new technology's effect on food production. As long as the petroleum supply holds out (or as renewable replacements are found), farmers will produce a constantly increasing supply of food, thanks to energy-intensive technological innovations such as irrigation and factory farming. But the ultimate effect is clear: The resulting population increase will eventually use up scarce natural resources, leading to the threat of irreversible environmental destruction.

Happily, there has been some success in controlling the human population explosion. The world population growth rate peaked at two percent in the late 1960s and is currently about 1.3 percent. Global average births are now 2.7 children per woman, down from five in the early 1950s.[4] This success is largely due to three things: (1) changes in lifestyle as development has occurred; (2) UN programs that provide access to birth control and family planning education to developing countries; and (3) the severe birth control policies in China, the world's most populous nation with 1.2 billion people. In 1979 the Chinese government mandated that each couple could have only one child—a drastic but effective way to control population growth.

Over 97 percent of the current population increase occurs in the developing world.[5] The developing world's lack of both education and access to birth control, as well as the low status of women, greatly contribute to the population explosion. Developed societies, on the other hand, have reached zero growth, i.e., the number of births about equals the number of deaths each year. When all the data are considered, the rate of growth and family size has been decreasing in both the developed and the developing parts of the world. Unfortunately, when you have a world population of 6.3 billion, even a small growth rate creates a large number of people. Each year there is an increase of 79 million people, about the size of the population of Germany or the Philippines. And, as noted earlier, increased longevity is also a key factor in the growth of populations. The question remains: Can population be stabilized sufficiently before the planet that sustains us all is irreversibly damaged? In the meantime, what can we do to reduce the tally of 24,000 people who die every day from hunger or hunger-related causes?

The first steps in managing population growth are to raise awareness of the problem and find the political will to deal with it as an international problem. In other words, *the solutions must be global because the problem itself is global.* It is not helpful to merely tighten up border controls to try to stop the flow of immigrants. The developed world needs to be proactive; it must endeavor to get to the root causes of the problem.

The UN has been instrumental in providing family planning assistance to developing nations, but it is limited by lack of funds. (The total UN budget for a year is $11 billion, compared to a US military budget of $400 billion.) The task of assisting developing countries requires not just family planning, but also clean water and adequate food and health care. The UN has made a good start, but a global government with a steady financial base could do so much more.

Also putting a brake on the UN's efforts in this direction —besides the general lack of funds—has been the particular lack of support from the UN's main contributor, the United States government. The US approach to world population control has for many years been lacking. For example, in 2002, the US withdrew $34 million from the United Nations Fund for Population Activities (UNFPA).[6] The successful domestic effort of the American Christian right to discredit global population control policy because of its use of family planning and abortion has been a key factor that has rendered the US largely ineffective on the critical issue of world population.

Ironically, while abortion is legal in America, US foreign policy involves dictating antiabortion policies to other countries. Under the current voluntary system of funding of the UN, countries can withhold payment for programs they don't like. Selective payment policies like these will be eliminated under the mandatory tax collection system of a democratic global government—just as it is with any government.

The so-called Global Gag Rule is the term often used to designate the US policy that denies foreign organizations receiving US family planning funds the right to engage in public debate on abortion or to perform legal abortions. The rule was originally proposed by the Reagan administration at the 1984 UN International Conference on Population in Mexico City. This policy remained in place from 1984 to 1993, ending during the eight years of the Clinton presidency, but it was reinstated by George W. Bush in 2001 on his first day in office as president. We know what works in controlling population growth: the provision of contraceptives, reproductive health and family planning services, clean water, health care, and incentives to limit family size; reduction of childhood mortality rates; and education for both men and women. In 1989 Iran faced water shortages and a population that had doubled from 1968 to 1988. It managed to institute a population control program that succeeded in reducing its birth rate. The Iranians used education and free access to birth control. Iran found the political will and translated it into effective programs that used financial incentives and social pressure. Cuba, with a population growth rate of only 0.7 percent[7] is another success story. The Cuban government provides family planning services at no cost to all citizens.

The developing world needs access to education, family planning, and technology. Women need to be given more rights and choices before they become pregnant. When the leaders and peoples of the world realize how greatly overpopulation affects the earth and everyone's well-being, the political will can be found to control it. But because we live in an interconnected and interdependent world, it does little good for one country to limit its population, only to be overrun by its neighbors. Population growth needs to be dealt with on a global level. The developed countries that have stabilized their population growth need to help the developing countries to also achieve this goal. Such policies can best be carried out by a democratic global government and especially by an end to war, which will free up the resources to do the job.

Global government is needed to address the AIDS epidemic

Infectious diseases know no borders, and thanks to modern transportation, deadly diseases can spread quickly and silently around the globe. The unchecked appearance of a mutant strain of virus or bacteria anywhere in the world can quickly become a threat to every one of us. The so-called avian influenza (or "bird flu") that recently struck in Southeast Asia is one such example that is currently causing great concern.

But no disease in modern times has been more devastating or has spread as fast as AIDS. The rate of increase of this disease since it was discovered in 1981 has been staggering, and scientists fear that we are only at the beginning of the most deadly plague known to humanity. As of 2004 AIDS had already claimed 24 million lives worldwide. It killed three million people in 2004, and five million more were newly infected. Worldwide it is estimated that about 40 million people are living with HIV/AIDS. Almost 30 million of those infected live in sub-Saharan Africa where the devastation is extensive.[8] Whole areas of this region have lost large segments of the adult population; in fact, UN officials now believe that AIDS is a major cause of Africa's current food crisis. It is a sign, they say, of how basic building blocks of society can crumble in the face of a devastating disease that urgently requires more global attention. Because AIDS is an international problem reaching into every corner of the globe, a huge international response is now needed.

What is needed most is an effective and inexpensive vaccine. Experts and activists have indicated that the amount of money and effort expended in that direction needs to be drastically increased.

In the meantime, it is essential to stop the spread of the disease through a simple, low-tech method: education for prevention. Nearly half of all new HIV infections and one-third of all new sexually transmitted infectious diseases occur to people younger than twenty-five. These young people need education, because AIDS is a preventable disease; it is not like the flu or tuberculosis, which can be contracted easily through the air. Condoms could be distributed free or their cost greatly subsidized to encourage safe sex. Intensive education programs on prevention should be stepped up in both the developed and the developing countries. As hundreds of millions of people may die in the next fifty years, these are not extreme ideas. The current uncoordinated approach is failing to stop or slow the epidemic.

When the world experienced an outbreak of Severe Acute Respiratory Syndrome (SARS) in 2003, the response was strong and involved mandatory quarantines. This strategy halted the disease without the benefit of either a vaccine or a cure. Although China, the nation with the most cases, stumbled at first, it eventually stepped up to the challenge. Had it not done so, and had it lost control of the disease, SARS would have spread throughout the world. Our great fear should be that the next outbreak of some new infectious disease might occur in a nation that does not react quickly enough or cannot control it within its own borders.

With the health of the world's peoples so interconnected, it makes sense to have a global government that could do so much more than the current World Health Organization to centralize the prevention and control of infectious diseases worldwide. No country could legitimately claim national sovereignty as a reason for not following international standards in this regard.

AIDS and the threat of other pandemics is yet another example of global problems that require a global focus. Only when the world stops spending its fortunes and genius on war will it find the will and resources to deal with such maladies as well as the overarching issue of the health and well-being of the world's people.

A solution to global warming is urgently needed

The planet has one atmosphere that is shared by all people and living things, and this vital resource is being threatened in a manner that cries out for a global remedy.

Scientists have confirmed that the decade of the 1990s was the warmest on record, and a full ten of the past twenty years have been among the warmest on record.[9] Overall, global temperature has risen one degree Fahrenheit in the last one hundred years, with the sharpest part of this rise occurring in the last twenty years. The warmest year on record was 1998, 2002 was the second warmest, 2001 was the third warmest, and 2004 was the fourth warmest according to the World Meteorological Organization. Most alarming is the prediction

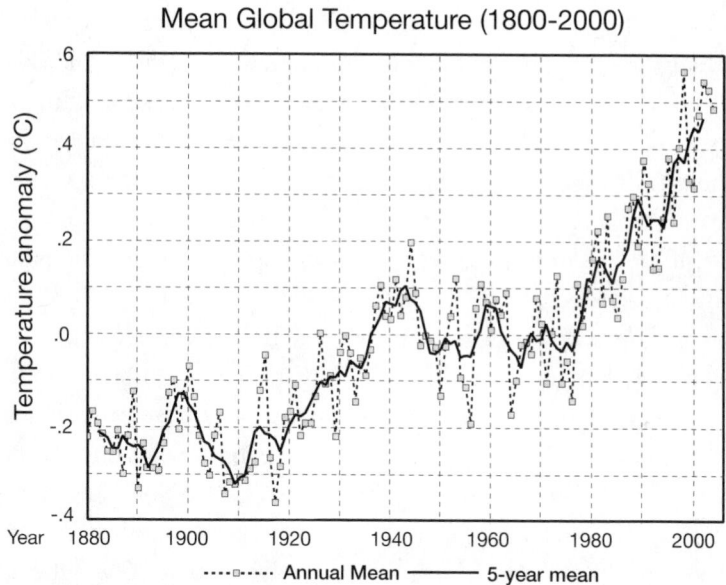

Mean Global Temperature (1800-2000)

····□···· Annual Mean ———— 5-year mean

Source: NASA

that global temperatures will rise by between 2.5 and 10 degrees Fahrenheit in this century.[10]

With the exception of a few ideologues lingering on in the US, the global warming that is evidenced by these numbers is no longer considered a theory by the world's scientific community; it is occurring and it is measurable.

The world is also experiencing a marked rise in storm activity due to the increased evaporation of water resulting from the higher temperatures. The trend toward a disruptive warming of the Pacific ocean-atmosphere system known as El Niño has also caused significant changes in weather patterns worldwide as well as the destruction of coral reefs. Also associated with global warming is the unprecedented rate of melting of polar glaciers. In turn, sea levels have begun to rise and are expected to continue rising for the next 500 years, inevitably flooding many of the earth's most populated areas.

The earth has been through many cycles of climate change over the millennia, but the last ten thousand years have been an exceptionally stable period in the earth's climate history. This stability seems to have been a key factor in humankind's development of civilization. A steady and predictable climate is critical for humanity's survival; the implications of the drastic climate changes we now anticipate are far-reaching.

The real danger is not so much the phenomenon of climate change itself, but the *rate* of change. The fragile biosphere that supports plants, animals, and human societies can be drastically disrupted by quick changes in temperature. Crop yields and farming in general also become less predictable. Scientists call this man-made destabilization of the atmosphere global *warming*, implying that it will be a gentle, steady increase in temperature—but it might be more accurate to use words like *baking, frying,* or *scorching*. The scary fact is that scientists don't know how severe the temperature increase might be in the coming decades; global climate change resulting from pollution won't necessarily occur in a slow, steady progression. We may reach a critical threshold at which point the warming process could suddenly leap forward, causing drastic temperature changes within a few years. With our knowledge thus limited, wisdom requires that we pursue a path of caution if humanity is going to safeguard the valuable resources of this planet. Scientifically speaking, it borders on insanity for humankind to be pumping vast quantities of greenhouse gases into the atmosphere and not expect *some* kind of change. It would be unconscionable for us to ignore this.

There will be both winners and losers in any scenario resulting from a rapid rise in the earth's temperature. The growing seasons of northern areas like Canada and Siberia will increase, and that may be to their benefit; other regions will face extreme weather changes that will make farming more difficult. The greatest losers may be the areas affected by killer heat waves, like the one in Chicago in 1995 that caused the deaths of five hundred people or the scorching summer of 2003 in Europe that caused over ten thousand heat-related deaths in France alone.[11] Meanwhile, tropical diseases like malaria will spread north; and food production all over the world will be disrupted by droughts and floods as weather patterns become even more unstable.

Global warming is caused primarily by the burning of fossil fuels, which emit carbon dioxide (the primary greenhouse gas), and by the clearing of forests. (Forests give off oxygen and absorb carbon dioxide, which stabilizes the climate.) Because of the developed world's massive dependence on fossil fuels, the carbon dioxide content in the atmosphere today is approximately 31 percent greater than it was in 1750 at the onset of the fossil-fuel era.[12] Carbon dioxide levels are now higher than at any time in the last 15 million years.[13]

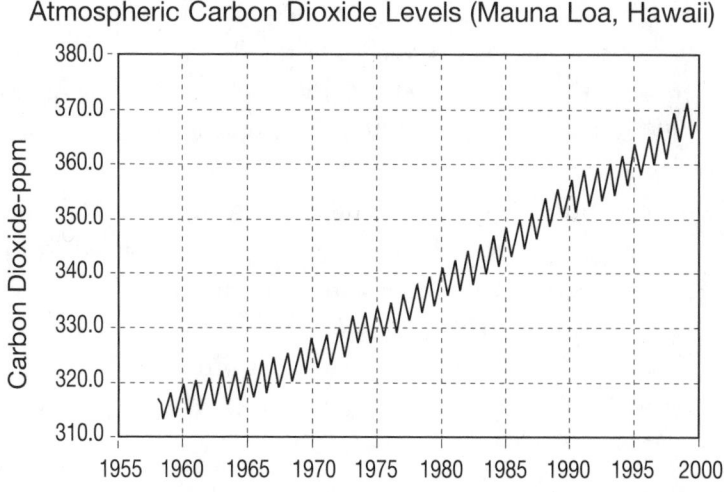

Atmospheric Carbon Dioxide Levels (Mauna Loa, Hawaii)

Source: Dave Keeling and Tim Whorf (Scripps Institution of Oceanography)

Fossil fuels are industrial society's main energy source. The cars we drive run on fossil fuel, our buildings are heated and cooled by fossil fuels, and most of the electricity that runs our homes and factories is created in plants that run on fossil fuels. The number of cars on the planet in 1950 was 50 million. In 2003 it was 500 million.[14] Countries that currently have few automobiles are increasingly emulating the US lifestyle and over time will drastically add to the total number of internal combustion engines producing greenhouse gases. We are expanding the fossil fuel bonanza with little regard for its environmental costs.

Global warming, like most problems, is easier to prevent than it is to fix. We have a window of opportunity in the next few years that will allow us to prevent a major catastrophe for the planet. People all over the world need to take action *now* to change energy-use patterns to prevent the future climate change that may create hardships for generations to come. Global warming can be confronted by changing the way we produce and use energy and by controlling population growth.

The world is attempting to deal with global warming through the Kyoto Protocol (1997), which formalized a voluntary set of agreements reached at the Rio Summit in 1992. Generally, the agreement entails limiting greenhouse gases to 1990 levels or below. In 2004, the world crossed a historic threshold with Russia's ratification of Kyoto, which, along with the ratifications of 130 other countries (excluding the US), turned the Kyoto Protocol into a formal treaty. But treaty law lacks a strong enforcement mechanism—and this planet's future is too important to rest on voluntary compliance and promises. A nation's right to do what it pleases ends when it negatively impacts other nations. Global government is the best way to handle the implementation of the laws necessary to address global warming. A democratic world legislature could mandate rules applicable to all countries that would describe permissible levels of emissions of greenhouse gases. These laws would be enforced by a world executive, while global courts would interpret the complexities of global environmental law. Through a democratic process that would engage the world's people, a global government could transform the ineffective Kyoto Protocol into enforceable law.

The world's environment is the life support system of the whole planet; it is a shared resource of all nations, and the peoples of this world are its sovereign. The control of this life support system can best be done in a coordinated manner by a democratic global government that creates rules that bring order out of chaos and promote the common good over the greed of the few.

Any scientist can testify that a dead ocean means a dead planet. . . . No national law, no national precautions can save the planet. The ocean, more than any other part of our planet . . . is a classic example of the absolute need for international, global action.

—Thor Heyerdahl

9

World Democracy
and the
Global Energy Crisis

My father rode a camel, I drive a car,
my son flies an airplane,
and his son will ride a camel.

—Arab saying

Fossil fuels pollute our environment and our bodies, are the direct cause of global warming, and are nonrenewable. At some point the oil and gas that makes the world economy run will become scarce and then eventually disappear. It is obvious that a sustainable global society cannot be built on such a finite resource.

We all know that industrial society is extremely dependent on oil to run motor vehicles, heat or cool living areas, generate electricity, transport staples, produce fertilizer—just about everything that makes our lives what they are. Cheap energy has, in fact, been the basis of the developed world's industrialization for well over a century. In the last chapter we noted that once the era of peak oil begins—which many experts say is imminent—disruptions will spread throughout the world economic system. Effective global government will be needed to adjudicate the conflicts that will inevitably arise, conflicts that could easily lead to "oil wars." (In fact, they already have several times, according to many accounts.) Peak oil is without doubt one of those global crises that cries out for a solution through the vehicle of democratic deliberation by the representatives of the world's peoples.

Developing countries everywhere are following in the footsteps of the advanced industrialized nations in basing their economies on fossil fuels. Those countries that are now industrializing, like China, will soon face fierce competition for dwindling oil supplies whose prices will be steadily climbing. Nearly a billion people in China are now changing from bicycles to cars and beginning to use refrigerators and other electrical devices. As a result, China has gone from an oil exporter to an oil importer in the last ten years and has replaced Japan in 2004 as the world's second largest consumer of oil after the US.[1] A similar process is happening around the world with other industrializing powers such as Brazil, and will reach a critical point in the near future.

As we saw in the last chapter, the luxury of affordable energy has allowed humankind to increase the carrying capacity of the earth to support a population of over six billion. By the same token, the impending loss of inexpensive energy will have far-reaching effects on populations everywhere. Economic output will slow and supplies will have to be rationed, creating personal hardships and lifestyle changes worldwide. Countries that still have exportable petroleum left will become increasingly powerful, and countries that are losers in the global competition for oil will experience energy shortages that may force a return to pre-industrial methods of living.

Global government must play a key role in renewables

Given the foregoing discussion, there can be no other conclusion: Alternative and renewable sources of energy—

many of which have long been available but whose potential has not yet been realized—need to be widely developed. This is an imperative for the global economy, not just to save the planet's environment, but also to protect industrial society from decline or collapse.

Currently available non-petroleum sources of energy, such as solar, wind, and hydroelectric power, are nonpolluting and inexhaustible. In Denmark, for example, 17 percent of electricity consumed in 2003 was generated by wind, and the cost of electricity in Denmark is lower than in many surrounding countries.[2] Germany has taken the lead on renewable energy development with large-scale use of solar and wind power. Why not follow that lead in the United States? The Great Plains of the US offers a potential wind-power gold mine. Wind power can be expanded with current technology to meet more of the demand for renewable energy, but like other renewables, it should be government-subsidized to compensate for its ability to reduce the costs of environmental pollution.

But wind, solar, and hydroelectric power have one big drawback compared to oil. To get oil, one only needs to drill a hole in the right place, and then sit back and tap years and years worth of stored solar energy. Relatively speaking, the cost of production is low and the return is high. In contrast, harnessing solar, wind, or water energy requires a much larger investment with a relatively lower return. This means either one of two things: We will need additional technologies or other sources of energy to supplement solar, wind, or water energy—or the planet will need to quickly become extremely efficient and ruthlessly conservative about energy use. Either way, a democratic global government would be a key ingredient in managing the solution.

Hydrogen is an option—
especially with a global approach

Hydrogen offers an option that must be explored as a candidate for replacing petroleum. Its chief benefit is that it is nonpolluting: When hydrogen is burned it combines with oxygen to create water as the only waste product; no carbon is added to the atmosphere.

Hydrogen can be used to run cars, heavy equipment—even airplanes. It can be burned directly or stored in a fuel cell, which acts as an electric generator. The fuel cell can store energy and be refueled; unlike a battery, it doesn't need constant replacement. Fuel cells also offer the advantage of being able to be linked together to form a network similar to today's power grid, so that energy surpluses and shortages can be equalized.

Hydrogen does have important drawbacks, however. It is never found in its free form in the environment, whereas oil and natural gas are. It can only be produced by using energy to split it from other atoms, as in separating it from oxygen in water. At the moment, most commercial hydrogen is extracted through a process called natural gas re-formation—that is, from natural gas, a fossil fuel. But supply of natural gas is limited; it contains carbon that gets released into the atmosphere as the hydrogen is harvested. Therefore, this approach is a poor choice for future hydrogen production.

Hydrogen can also be liberated by the electrolysis of water into hydrogen and oxygen, a process that requires electricity. The source of the input electricity is the critical factor in this approach. If it were produced solely from renewable, nonpolluting sources, such as sun or wind, then one would have a complete cycle of low-impact energy generation and storage. The real question thus becomes: How much clean hydrogen can reasonably be generated in this way—and at what cost? It takes energy and money to create other forms of energy. Every time one form of energy is converted to another form (for example, using coal-derived electricity to produce hydrogen), energy is lost in the process and costs are incurred.

The sad truth is that replacing coal-derived energy with renewables as the input is not now economically feasible; in other words, the cost-benefit ratio is not there for creating a wind- or solar-based system able to generate the amount of hydrogen needed to run an economy. It is a question of economies of scale. There is no current scenario that would allow us to accomplish such a feat on a large enough scale to generate anything near to what oil yields in energy output. But such a scenario might be possible with the kind of resources and planning that could be supplied by a global government. And it might become our best option as the price of oil inevitably rises.

Hydrogen does offer great promise in the short run as a *medium* of energy—that is, for storing and transferring it. However, it is not a viable *source* of energy at the moment. Fuel-cell cars that are powered by hydrogen are actually running on the electricity that created the hydrogen. If that electricity comes from a coal-fired power plant, then the car is essentially running on coal. The hydrogen fuel-cell car is cleaner because it doesn't produce carbon dioxide or other pollutants that come out the tailpipe, but unless the source of electricity it is running on comes from a less-polluting renewable energy source, such as wind or solar, it offers no improvement.

A global government could mount an "Energy Marshall Plan"

One promising form of energy is fusion-based nuclear power, but like hydrogen and the renewables, liberating its potential may require global government.

When nuclear power based on fission (the splitting of the atom) was first invented, people thought it a panacea—an almost unlimited and cheap source of power. They were wrong. Nuclear power turned out to be neither cheap nor plentiful. The cost of building and maintaining plants proved to be prohibitive when the safety and environmental factors were included.

Furthermore, nuclear power plants represent disasters waiting to happen. A complete meltdown at a nuclear plant could kill or injure millions. And the reality is that terrorists do not have to build their own nuclear weapons in order to terrorize a country—vulnerable nuclear power plants exist all over the developed world! Every nuclear plant is like a large "dirty bomb" just waiting for a terrorist to activate it. Nuclear power plants also produce plutonium, an essential ingredient of nuclear weapons that could easily fall into the hands of a terrorist organization. Some experts believe this has already happened.

The other big drawback to nuclear energy is the radioactive waste that is produced at every plant. We have no way to recycle this waste or destroy its toxicity.

Fortunately, the US recognized the dangers of nuclear power after the Three Mile Island accident and stopped building new plants years ago. (No new ones have been ordered since 1978.) But they are still being built in other parts of the world. In a responsible world, one led by a democratic government, all existing nuclear power plants would be decommissioned for the safety of the people living near them. By eliminating nuclear power plants worldwide, the spread of nuclear weapons will also be kept in check, since it takes a nuclear power plant to produce plutonium, the essential ingredient of nuclear weapons.

But there is still a future for nuclear energy: The current technology of nuclear *fission* can be replaced with more efficient nuclear *fusion*. Fission involves splitting atoms from highly radioactive uranium molecules, while fusion is the combining of hydrogen atoms to make helium atoms. Fusion is the same reaction that powers the sun. Fusion, once perfected, would run on hydrogen, which is found in water, instead of uranium. Fusion does not produce nuclear waste. It is a much safer process and has the potential for delivering the promise of energy in abundance.

Scientists have been working on perfecting the necessary electromagnetic fields and energy input needed to start and maintain the fusion reaction, but they are not yet there. It requires time, money, and planning—all in short supply.

But if the will existed and if scientists were put to work on energy projects such as fusion or hydrogen, instead of developing weapons, the world could free itself from fossil fuels and spur economic development in a sustainable way. We need the intensity of the Manhattan Project, which developed the atomic bomb, to solve the fusion problem and other challenges of renewable and nonpolluting energy sources— and thereby change our energy usage forever. Using the coordination of a global government, there is no doubt that the resources of many nations could be brought together so that scientists and engineers worldwide could work in harmony to develop new energy sources that would benefit the planet and all its inhabitants.

The role of energy
conservation is critical

Even if new energy technology does not assume the leading role, our energy use could be reshaped and the planet rendered sustainable through world government legislation that would mandate or encourage energy conservation.

The amount of energy squandered in just one part of the world—the United States—is tremendous. Having developed the automobile, Americans then proceeded to design their economic system and their entire lives around motor vehicles. Today most Americans are totally dependent on their cars, as typified by this scene: Just to buy a quart of milk, the average person has to fire up a two-ton vehicle and move it at least a mile. This is absurdly inefficient as the era of peak oil approaches. Suburban living may suddenly become rather inconvenient as gasoline prices rise to three or four dollars or even higher per gallon.

But the rigorous application of well-known techniques of energy conservation could make a huge difference. National legislation mandating conservation measures, and farsighted policies including improved zoning laws, better mass transportation, and other well-known approaches would all allow Americans to greatly reduce their dependence on fossil fuels. Important strides have already been made in Europe, where gasoline is taxed heavily, mass transit is efficient, and bicycles are more commonly used as everyday transportation.

Much of the problem for the US is corrupt politics. All too often, car manufacturers and oil companies are allowed to dictate American energy policy, as is typified by Vice President Cheney's notorious energy task force meetings. These companies run massive lobbies in Washington, and offer huge campaign donations to members of Congress and the

President, who in turn provide legislation and even prosecute wars that favor continued dependence on oil.

Again, the first and easiest step in changing America's energy policy would be to mandate conservation. One illustrative example is the humble solar hot-water heater. Consumers are reluctant to spend a lot of money up front for these devices. But when solar hot-water heaters were required by building codes, as they were in parts of the US in the late 1970s, many were installed. When the federal government gave a tax credit for half the cost of a solar hot-water system, they sold well. The point is that some energy-saving devices will not get used unless they are required by law—local laws, national laws, and someday global law.

Hybrid cars now on the market have price tags similar to those of standard gas vehicles, and they get a small government tax credit. However, without mandatory increases in gasoline fuel efficiency, they will remain a small part of the market. Government needs to take a leading role in creating energy standards and regulating energy usage. Leaving energy conservation to market forces has given us the SUV—a shortsighted vehicle choice that is emblematic of the great crisis that approaches.

The best way for government to encourage conservation is through financial incentives. As in Europe, energy use should be taxed to encourage conservation and the proceeds used to develop a more energy-efficient society. The world cannot rely on the market to correct its energy problems. The market has no regard for pollution costs and lacks the foresight to predict major shortages. It should be government's job to regulate energy usage for the greater good of society and the environment. We also need leaders to stand up to special interests in favor of public interests, as well as the good of the planet.

A global solution to
the energy crisis is needed

Oil depletion and global warming are now entering a critical period. The industrial nations need to act aggressively to change their energy production and usage habits, and they need to plan wisely, for it takes many years to retool society. Facing this challenge will be like steering the *Titanic* away from an iceberg; the ship's captain will want plenty of time to make the course correction because the ship is huge and unwieldy. But very little time is left.

In summary, a few things are obvious to all observers: Solar and wind power need to be greatly expanded and further developed. Research into all other types of clean energy generation, especially hydrogen and fusion, needs to be expanded, and conservation efforts should be dramatically stepped up worldwide.

The planet is now facing an inexorable energy crisis. With an inevitable decline in oil supplies, and a looming environmental catastrophe resulting from global warming—a global government is needed now, among other things, to serve as a referee during the inevitable scrambling for resources and the finger-pointing among nations over who is at fault for the disaster. The peoples' world government would decide how disputes are resolved and make sure they are fought in courts, not on battlefields.

To deal with the crisis itself, a global government could create rules regarding energy usage and carbon emissions that apply equally to all countries and are legally binding and enforced by the power of global law. Global government could concentrate scientific resources to address the shared challenges of the coming energy shortage. And, most importantly, global government would play a crucial role in forestalling the wars that otherwise will occur as nations compete for shrinking supplies of oil and other resources. The inevitable energy crisis is high on the list of the many serious global problems that require a momentous global solution.

> *Science has made unrestricted national sovereignty incompatible with human survival. The only possibilities are now world government or death.*
>
> —Bertrand Russell

10

Overcoming Poverty
through Global
Government

The mother of revolution and crime is poverty.
—Aristotle

One of the key functions of government is to take care of people who cannot take care of themselves, especially when nongovernmental solutions are simply not available. Where people find themselves in dire need—whether from a disaster such as an earthquake or flood, or due to poverty, famine, or disease—it falls to government to coordinate the redistribution of resources to alleviate the suffering. Such humanitarian missions are ideally handled in cooperation with charities and NGOs (nongovernmental organizations) that focus on such needs. But in those all-too-common situations where such public interest institutions are absent, or when their capabilities for service are overwhelmed, it is government that must step in as the provider of last resort. Sometimes, as in the South Asian tsunami calamity of December 2004, only the resources of the largest governments are in a position to manage the enormity of the disaster.

In less dire situations, local, state, and national governments routinely provide disaster relief and all manner of support services to the poor and disabled in the developed world. But in the developing world, because so many national governments are inadequate or corrupt, the fundamental governmental task of taking care of those who cannot take care of themselves often goes unfulfilled, with tragic consequences.

On every continent, national governments are forced by the global war system to spend inordinate amounts of money on their armed forces, draining their treasuries of precious funds needed for basic services. Corruption, inefficiency, and lack of infrastructure further impede these societies. What can be done in such countries to alleviate the poverty, disease, or famine that is occurring right now?

Under the current global system, the only resources available to ease the massive amount of suffering and poverty in the developing world come from small amounts of international charity or foreign aid, under-funded UN programs, or inadequate assistance donated by the international community when crises arise that are dire enough to attract world media attention.

The result is a world in which many basic human needs, such as water, food, shelter, and medical treatment, go unmet—a morally repugnant spectrum of widespread and routine violations of fundamental human rights.

The world must address the preventable problems of the poor

In a most profound way, this planet is divided into the haves and the have-nots. Most citizens of so-called developed countries have little knowledge of how the rest of the world lives. Currently, over a billion people survive on less than a dollar a day and almost three billion on less than two dollars. Two-thirds of the poor are women and children. Every year, 10 million people die from poverty-related causes.

When looking at the statistics for preventable problems in the developing countries, one finds numbers that are staggering. Millions of people die simply as a result of contaminated water; all sorts of preventable and curable diseases kill millions each year. This information barely makes headlines. We see a plane crash and say that it is a tragedy, which it is. A much larger tragedy is going on every day, all over the world. Yet we ignore easily correctable problems such as clean water and disease prevention that kill millions.

Modern famines have occurred in Somalia, Ethiopia, and Bangladesh, just to name a few. These tragedies are usually caused by a variety of factors that include war, anarchy, drought, flood, overpopulation, deforestation, and political corruption. Poor countries have little reserves of food and money and are easily pushed over the edge by war, disease, or drought. The developed world has sometimes responded in such emergencies, but it has usually been too little, too late.

The UN has been instrumental in rebuilding nations after wars and disasters. It created a new government and developed infrastructure in Bosnia, after its war, as well as in East Timor. It has played a critical role in the development of Afghanistan after the US overthrew the Taliban. But lack of funds severely limits what the UN can do.

The task is immense. Dealing with preventable problems of the world's poor countries requires far more resources than are currently available to the UN. True prevention requires "teaching a man how to fish." Developing health and prosperity in deprived areas of the world requires educating people, providing the capital and tools they need to build society, and empowering them to act in new ways through democratic institutions. Donated money is helpful, but so much more is needed. If needy people merely receive money without learning how to create their own wealth, the money will quickly disappear. (This is why 80 percent of lottery winners are broke in three years.) People can raise themselves out of poverty if they are given hope, education, and opportunity.

The Peace Corps is probably the best model of how outsiders from the West can help people to help themselves. It provides education and resources to developing nations so communities can improve their agricultural production, health care, and infrastructure. It is much more effective to use the Peace Corps to prevent famines than to send in humanitarian assistance after the fact. But institutions like the Peace Corps are also limited by a lack of money and resources.

Billionaire Bill Gates donated one billion dollars to the World Health Organization, gave $100 million to develop an AIDS vaccine, and has pledged to give a total of $3.2 billion to improve health care in developing countries. Gates has said, "All you have to do is take a modest amount of the rich world's resources to have a huge impact on the poor world."[1] He looked at the statistics, saw for himself the suffering around the world, and recognized that improving people's health was the place to start. Gates has also stated that the capitalist system has failed to bring medicine to the developing world, and that in fact drug companies do not develop treatments or vaccines for the diseases of the developing world because there is no profit in it.[2] His donation shows us a way to begin: We need to help people in developing countries get healthy enough to have the energy to solve their other problems. Poverty and many diseases can be eliminated worldwide. The people of the world have the means—we just need the political will to do it.

Fighting global poverty
is in everyone's interest

Helping the suffering peoples of the world is not just an altruistic act. It is in everyone's self-interest in an interconnected and interdependent world.

Despite the reality that the world is really one global civilization, we live in a world that lacks the binding force of global law. In this condition of relative anarchy, political instability and economic inequality are inevitable; these will in turn drive immigration as well as terrorism. History shows that failed or weak states easily become breeding grounds for unrest that can spill over borders. One clear example is the case of Afghanistan: The US abandoned any interest in the country after the withdrawal of the Soviet forces in the early 1980s. The hapless Afghans then went through years of anarchy and civil war only to come under the domination of the Taliban. These new rulers were indebted to Osama bin Laden, offering him and al Qaeda a safe haven. Not long after, the people of US unfortunately learned on September 11, 2001, that our neglect of the poorest countries in the developing world has consequences.[3]

It is difficult to maintain a peaceful world if billions of people are hungry and deprived. Furthermore, when people live in poverty, they tend to destroy the environment for short-term gains, specifically personal survival. For example, the gathering of firewood by millions of people who need it to heat their homes and cook their food has led to deforestation throughout the developing world, and deforestation is believed to be one of the causes of global warming. This is yet another reason why it is in the developed world's own self-interest to eradicate poverty in the developing world.

Improved health in the developing world would lower infant mortality rates, which, in turn, would lower birth rates. When people know their children are likely to survive, they choose to have fewer. This phenomenon can be seen around the world: In the developed world, where health care is available, the birth rate has come down to replacement levels. If we can do the same in the developing world, much of the pressure comes off the related problems of poverty and instability that directly affect all of us.

Global government is the only effective solution to global poverty

When one lives under a stable system of law, the burden of taking care of people unable to take care of themselves is shared equally by the functioning members of society operating through democratic government. Realistically speaking, the UN, the Peace Corps, and Bill Gates—as helpful as they have been—are capable of making only a dent in the enormous tragedy of billions of people living in poverty. Solving the problem in an organized and consistent manner can come only through the response of government, particularly global government.

A democratic world federal government would make poverty the concern of all countries. It would use its income from taxes to fight worldwide poverty and would not have to beg for the payment of "dues" as the UN does now. Once people understand that weapons can't create peace—and that only enforceable global law can prevent war and preparations for war—then the world will shift its spending priorities to programs that address the dire conditions of the world's neediest. The elimination of national military budgets would free up vast financial resources to address poverty and hunger.

The economic imbalances of the world must be addressed for the sake of creating a peaceful and environmentally stable world. We cannot consider ourselves civilized and yet allow the widespread misery of hunger and treatable diseases to flourish on our planet. A global government is by far the best vehicle for dealing with failed states, and for settling the conflicts and civil wars that rage around the world and cause some of the most acute humanitarian crises. A democratic government of humankind is our best hope for creating effective programs for the elimination of poverty and reducing needless suffering on our planet.

*It is a tragic mix-up when the United States
spends $500,000 for every enemy soldier killed, and
only $53 annually on the victims of poverty.*
—Martin Luther King, Jr.

11

The Need to Rethink Borders

*World federalists hold before us the vision of a
unified mankind living in peace under a just
world order. . . . The heart of their program—a
world under law—is realistic and attainable.*

—U Thant
Former UN Secretary-General

In the first chapter we discussed the breathtaking image
of the earth as seen from deep space by the Apollo astronauts,
and we also allude to it on the cover of this book. Now bring
yourself back to this pristine image and the serene moment
experienced by the Apollo crew upon seeing the earth as a
whole for the first time. Notice the obvious fact that our sphere
of habitation is completely lacking in lines of political separation. Remind yourself that these so-called national borders are
the creations of the human mind—they are nothing more than
political artifacts that often serve to divide humanity. We have
made borders into instruments of abuse and repression, and in
this chapter we will envision how we can *unmake* them.

In an era where national sovereignty reins supreme, borders may mark a country's sovereign territory but they also
divide ordinary human beings from one another; they contribute to the delusion that humanity is not truly "one people."
They create an "us" versus "them" mentality that can lead to

war. A border can also function to the detriment of the commerce and culture of populations on each side of it, who often have more in common with each other than they know. Borders ultimately create the illusion of national sovereignty—when in reality sovereignty belongs to the people of the world in relation to the planet as a whole.

Politicians and dictators alike have understood borders to be a proper line of defense for a country, and thus for several millennia people have raised armies to hold the line and keep invaders out. Borders permit the control of trade and especially today offer a way to control the flow of immigrants, illegal drugs, and terrorists. National borders may also define the presence of a particular culture, although this notion is barely viable in today's interconnected global society. At its worst, some countries use borders like the walls of a prison to keep their own citizens in. Throughout the last century communist regimes routinely used borders to abuse their populations. When in 1961 East Germany built the Berlin Wall, this border became a global symbol of the struggle for the right of free passage.

Borders in the era of global democratic government will become more like the borders between states or provinces. Paradoxically, a world government will empower local and national governments to handle their own problems by removing the burden of large military expenditures and providing development assistance. In other words, global problems will finally be handled at the global level based on the sovereignty of the world's people; national and local problems will be handled where *they* occur based on the principle of self-determination and subsidiarity. This "democratic new world order" will allow the free movement of world citizens, ideas, and commerce around the globe.

Borders in today's world of relative anarchy too often lead to human suffering. For example, many people die every year trying to get into the United States; whether it be Cubans and Haitians on small boats, Chinese on cargo ships, or Mexicans in trucks, the inability of people to emigrate and travel freely is a human tragedy. The US and many other countries are still living down the shame of denying admittance to millions of Jews who were fleeing the Holocaust and had to face the gas chambers instead. There are still many stateless refugees who have left their countries due to war or other threats of harm, such as the millions of Afghans who left their country during the twenty years of its civil war, or the millions of Palestinians still living without a sovereign government. With few countries willing to take in refugees, many such stateless people live in temporary camps without full rights of citizenship. In a world governed by law under the sovereignty of humankind, these people would always carry with them their constitutionally guaranteed rights as world citizens.

In a society with open borders, countries would be more engaged in the world and its problems. Our false sense of security and artificial attitude of isolation would disappear. No country can be safe if the rest of the world is in turmoil. In reality, all countries and peoples of the world are interdependent and interconnected. We are all in this together no matter what nationality we call ourselves—our fates are one.

As a global federation is formed, countries within the federation will naturally reduce or eliminate border restrictions, and this will be made possible by the increased sense of security resulting from life under the rule of law. Yes, borders will still exist as the defining lines between countries. They will mark where one government is in charge versus another and they will indicate where a particular set of laws applies in accord with national traditions of governance. But these borders will be open, just as the borders between counties or provinces within a country are open. A global democratic government will have the power to guarantee freedom of passage around the world and regulate the resettlement of refugees according to law. It will also guarantee that all human beings have a basic right to leave their country of origin and to return to it, ensuring that no country becomes a prison for its citizens.

Migration and trade issues need a global solution

There is generally little pressure for people to migrate between countries with similar levels of political freedom and standards of living. For example, when the borders of the original EU countries were opened up, there were no major migrations. But with the recent addition to the EU of Eastern European countries, migration to the West is now occurring.

With populations increasing dramatically in the developing countries, we can expect that migration to the developed world will become a more pressing issue in the future. The US-Mexico border is a prime example of a meeting place between these two worlds. The US offers jobs, educational opportunities, and a lifestyle that act as a magnet pulling people in. The result: The US has approximately eight to nine million illegal immigrants living within its borders and receives about 500,000 illegal immigrants per year, according to US Census Bureau estimates.[1] Even with a border that has been greatly strengthened and militarized by the US through the implementation of Operation Gatekeeper, people still risk death to get from Mexico to the United States.

US policy towards Mexican immigration is a confused and contradictory assemblage of laws. The US occasionally gives amnesty and rarely prosecutes employers of illegal work-ers. In reality, some of these so-called illegal aliens are needed because they do jobs Americans are not willing to do, such as farm labor.

Meanwhile, vast amounts of money are spent to defend this porous border. These resources would be better spent get-ting to the heart of the problem: overpopulation, poverty, and corruption in Mexico and other developing countries. The best thing the US could do to stem the tide of immigrants coming from Mexico and other developing countries would be to launch a massive campaign of foreign aid for development, political reform, and family planning assistance to Mexico and the rest of the developing world. Only by creating economic opportunities and empowering people in the developing countries will tension on the border be reduced. Putting up concrete and barbed wire doesn't help either side.

The approval of the North American Free Trade Agreement (NAFTA) by Canada, the US, and Mexico in 1994 created a freer trade policy between these three countries, and was hailed as a step toward more open borders for large corporations. Similar legislation to extend free trade policies to all countries in the Western Hemisphere, excepting Cuba, is now under negotiation. While such free trade agreements are important in creating a global society, it is crucial that provi-sions be included that ensure labor rights and environmental protection for the member nations. Under NAFTA, many US corporations move their operations to Mexico simply to avoid environmental regulation in the US. That represents a step backward for both peoples. A democratic world government would create uniform global laws that would regulate world trade—and especially the behavior of multinational corpora-tions, wherever they operate.

The EU is setting the stage
for more open borders

Are open borders realistic? One need only look to Europe to answer that question. Borders similar to those between states in the US still exist among EU members, but these countries have drastically reduced or eliminated border restrictions, with positive results. The EU uses a controlled process that minimizes massive population movements, beginning with easing of restrictions and economic assistance and progressing to open borders. People, money, and commerce now move more easily between countries. A citizen of the EU can now live or work anywhere in the EU. The elimination of border restrictions is a remarkable achievement on a continent that was once the worst killing field of the twentieth century.

Europe has set an example by showing that border restrictions can be eased through peaceful negotiations. But in order to open up borders worldwide to achieve international peace and prosperity, the world must first find ways to reduce tensions among nations that cause excessive migration or even infiltration by terrorists. The causes of international friction—poverty, rapid population growth, war, and political corruption and repression—must be addressed by the organized response of a global government.

In the meantime, one way to begin reducing cross-border tensions and the terrorist threat is for America—the world's richest and most influential country—to cut its military budget and expand its foreign development aid budget. The embarrassing fact is that US government foreign aid is a tiny fraction of the Pentagon's budget. The US needs to realize that having prosperous and stable neighbors is crucial in an interdependent world in which one country's problems quickly become another's. Foreign aid can spur the development of prosperous, democratic, peace-loving societies; one need only look at what the US did to remake Japan and Europe after World War II. The Marshall Plan in Europe created a democratic Western Europe out of rubble. Japan was also rebuilt into an economic and democratic powerhouse. Sadly, the US has forgotten this lesson. It is now focused on military "defense" rather than empowering the people of the developing countries, to its own and the world's detriment.

The world is localizing and globalizing at the same time

The redrawing of borders to create new or expanded political entities has been going on since the beginning of recorded history. National borders are still unstable in some regions, as new countries are created or existing boundaries are changed through civil war or other means. Many countries continue to suffer from ongoing border disputes, either with other countries or, more typically, with separatist groups within their own borders. As a global federation gains power, it will play a major role in settling these disputes throughout the world.

Racial, ethnic, and cultural groups all over the world crave autonomy—from Quebec to Palestine to Chechnya. No country, people, or tribe wants to be controlled by another group. This same desire for self-determination has been the force behind decolonization around the world, including the independence of America from Britain more than two centuries ago. In the decades after WWII, many colonies, such as Algeria, India, and Vietnam, just to name a few, fought for and won their independence. The Soviet Union's recent breakup into independent nations in a relatively short period of time was one of the most significant political events of the last fifty years.

Separatist movements can be sources of bloody conflict, as witnessed in the war in Chechnya and the breakup of Yugoslavia in the 1990s. As more groups around the world demand autonomy, the inevitable disputes will require a world court with the power to enforce its decisions to keep the peace. For example, a world court could play a constructive, lifesaving role in settling the ongoing dispute over Kashmir between two nuclear powers, India and Pakistan.

A genuine world court would also provide the best solution to the most intractable and dangerous dispute of our time, the Israeli-Palestinian conflict. A global government could order the parties to adjudicate the conflict by bringing evidence and arguments before the finest jurists in the world, who would then impose a settlement on the basis of the legitimacy of global law. When issues like these can be settled by the rule of law rather than by the rule of force, the world will have taken a great step forward.

The often just demands of such groups for self-determination do tend to fragment sovereignty. But the desire for independence does not preclude these new entities from coming together in cooperation at a global level. The UN started with fifty countries and now has 191 members, and many of these new members are countries that were created after the founding of the UN. By the same token, Eastern European nations that recently gained independence are just as quickly joining the European Union. Even NATO has expanded greatly in the years since the breakup of the Soviet Union. (It now includes countries that used to be part of the

Soviet bloc, such as Poland, Romania, and even countries that were part of the Soviet Union, such as Estonia and Latvia.) Our world is moving toward increased local control, free trade, and more open borders, while at the same time countries are increasingly seeking international protection and improvements in the enforcement of international law, such as the Kyoto Treaty or the ICC.

Paradoxically, the world is becoming more representative of true interests at the local level, yet politics and law are "going global." This pattern of development is leading toward a functional global government. Imagine this: The representatives to the coming world legislature will hail from hundreds of states and other jurisdictions. Their territorial integrity will be upheld or peacefully adjusted by the world government through which they create global legislation!

Even after a functioning world court under a global constitution exists—or *because* one comes into existence—some countries will be broken apart as a result of the demands of separatist movements. These people will want local control of local issues, but they will also ask for the protection of the federation of nations. A global government, if intelligently designed and implemented, could provide that protection while allowing local freedom.

As we have noted in a previous chapter, the orderly and peaceful integration of different levels of legitimate sovereignty is the genius of the idea of world federation. By lawfully settling the territorial and border disputes of the world's nations one at a time and by creating peace between neighbors, we can build a world based on reason and law rather than on might and anarchy.

There's only one truth on this planet: that we
are all one. What I'd like to do before I die is bring
people closer to the same reality that John Coltrane
and Bob Marley were trying to bring people to—
a reality of no borders, one race, one body, where
we all take responsibility that nobody starves
to death tomorrow morning.

—Carlos Santana

12

The Critical Role
of the US in
Global Governance

*The United States . . . is the heir of a Western
civilization which has long been preoccupied with
the art and science of government. If the United
States does not take the initiative, no one will.*
—Albert Einstein

The US was most powerful at its founding, long before it had great armies and vast wealth. Its power came from the profound ideas it carried to the world: constitutional democracy, freedom of speech and religion, federalism, separation of church and state, and a system of checks and balances on power. By institutionalizing these ideas in the American constitution, the founders created the momentum that eventually laid waste to monarchies and tyranny throughout the world, creating the democratic age in which we now live. And many of these same concepts of governance will survive to become the cornerstones of the coming global constitution.

But America's role in the world has changed after two centuries. Tragically, it is now a widely held view around the world that our vast economic and military power has turned the US into a corrupt and self-serving superpower. International polls confirm that people throughout the world, and especially sizeable majorities in many European countries, believe that what the US now brings to the world is often not to the world's benefit. Especially under the current Bush regime, America has given lip service to diplomacy, cooperation, and international law—but in practice embraces unilateralism and the concept of might makes right over the rule of law.

While it advocates ridding the world of the threat of WMDs, the United States actually possesses more weapons of mass destruction than any other country and maintains the largest military force in the world.[1] It has spent over $14 trillion on its military forces since World War II, thereby generating a vast, self-serving, military-industrial-intelligence complex, and the massive Pentagon bureaucracy that manages it.[2] The US share of worldwide defense spending is about 40 percent—and that equals the next nine countries combined.[3]

It was the philosopher Nietzsche who once said, "When all you have is a hammer, your problems look like nails." America's hammer is its military might. The US under the Bush administration treats far too many complex global problems as if they are nails that need to be hammered with brute force instead of diplomacy. At this moment in history, America has bought into the war system more than any other major power, becoming its major upholder in the world. Sadly, this attitude probably makes America the greatest obstacle to the realization of a democratic world government—which is the only long-term cure for the war system that has resulted from the chaos of unlimited national sovereignty.

Let's look for a moment at the wide expanse of the American empire: The US Special Operations Forces, for just one example, are involved in military training, antinarcotics programs, antiterrorist activities, and equipment transfers, and are deployed in more than 140 countries with a budget of over $3 billion.[4] The US has regular troops stationed in every corner of the globe and at this moment is fighting two wars in the world's most volatile region.

While it speaks in high tones of "spreading liberty," America actually pursues a Machiavellian foreign policy, in effect saying, "We don't care if they hate us, as long as they fear us." Ironically, this hatred of America has now become the gravest threat to US citizens, especially in the way that our aggressive behavior in the Middle East and our support for Israel and Saudi Arabia has inflamed radical Islamists.

One of the reasons America is detested in some parts of the world is its policy of supporting dictators that favor US interests over the interests of the people who have to live under these brutal regimes. In some cases, the US has done even worse than merely support dictators—it actually *installed* them in the first place, sometimes replacing democratic regimes with tyrannical ones that favored US interests. The US helped overthrow the democratically elected government of Salvador Allende, a socialist in Chile, and replaced him with the brutal dictatorship of General Pinochet. The CIA played a decisive role in overthrowing Iran's democratically elected president in 1953, installing the Shah of Iran as ruler, and staunchly supported his repressive regime. In the late 1980s the US supported and armed Iraq's Saddam Hussein in his war with Iran. When Iraq was losing, the US sold Saddam chemical weapons, which he used against Iran's troops as well as against Iraqi Kurds. And there are many other cases of similar conduct on virtually every continent.

The US currently props up the Saudi royal family who rules Saudi Arabia, one of the world's most notoriously repressive and undemocratic regimes. There is an unholy alliance between America, the world's largest consumer of oil, and Saudi Arabia, the world's largest producer of oil, some of it brokered by the Bush family itself. While proclaiming the need for democratic values in the Middle East, America remains silent about a country where women cannot drive cars, only one religion is allowed, public beheadings take place, and dissent is not tolerated.

We could enumerate other examples of US manipulation of governments around the world, but authors like Noam Chomsky have already provided the full description. The simple moral of the story is this: The country that first brought democratic ideals to the world should actually be *supporting these ideals* around the world. Aside from working for enforceable global law, perhaps the best way the US could support the evolution of democracy overseas is by helping countries pull themselves out of poverty. But the US only gives about $13 billion yearly in total development aid worldwide. Of that amount, $3 billion goes to Israel and $2 billion to Egypt as part of the payoff for the 1979 peace deal between those two countries, leaving only about $8 billion for the rest of the world.[5] As we previously noted, this is a pittance compared to US military expenditure. America gives the least amount of development aid as a percentage of its gross national product of any industrialized country, and the Department of Defense has a budget fifteen times that of the Department of State. The fact that the US is constantly behind in paying its UN dues is a reflection of American priorities. At the end of August 2003, members owed the UN $2.3 billion, of which the United States alone owed $1.2 billion.

Nearly fifteen years after end of the Cold War, the US has not yet produced a sensible strategy in international relations.

Despite having the greatest military machine in the world and thousands of nuclear weapons, it was unable to protect US citizens against the terrorist attacks of September 11, 2001. America has now reached a point where it is spending untold billions of dollars on military forces that actually have the effect of making its citizens, and the rest of the world, less safe.

America is currently not ready to lead the world

America has always been a deeply individualistic society. It is the most competitive and capitalistic of the developed Western nations. It is the only developed country that allows the death penalty and the only one lacking a national health plan. It has the highest rate of infant mortality, the highest murder rate, and the most homeless people. No democratic country in the world has a higher percentage of its population in prison. These are not appropriate "leadership" characteristics for a country that is the world's sole superpower. It is clear that drastic reforms are needed in the US, both domestically and in foreign policy, before it is in a position to lead the world into the era of a democratic world government with a strong emphasis on human rights!

The US is also vulnerable economically. For example, when it comes to petroleum consumption, America is the world's biggest glutton: Though it has only 5 percent of the world's population, it consumes 25 percent of the world's oil.[6] US domestic oil production peaked in 1970 and has been in decline ever since.[7] Oil imports supplied 57 percent of US needs in 2001, compared to 47 percent a decade earlier and only 36 percent in 1981.[8] Oil is America's Achilles' heel. The US is a mighty giant with an addiction and a strategic weakness. With oil supply about to peak and the last great reserves sitting under the sands of the Persian Gulf, it is no wonder that America is aggressively and illegally defending its vital interests in this area.

America's foreign policy reflects its fundamental individualism through the unilateralist foreign policies of both Democratic and Republican administrations. In 1983 President Reagan invaded Grenada, and he bombed Libya in 1986. Both were violations of international law. In 1986, the US was condemned in the World Court for unlawful use of force when it mined Nicaraguan harbors; it ignored the court's judgment. In 1989, the first President Bush invaded Panama, causing approximately 300 civilian deaths, in violation of international law; the US then vetoed a resolution condemning the US action in the UN Security Council.[9] In 1998, President Clinton launched cruise missiles against Iraq in violation of international law. And in 2003, the second President Bush invaded Iraq as a preemptive measure against a perceived threat of WMDs, ignoring the clearly stated opposition of the world community. The claim that Saddam Hussein had WMDs was later disproved.

Such examples of unilateralism show why the US is a major obstacle to the development of global law. America appears to believe in a double standard: It expects other countries to abide by international law, but it currently views itself as being above such laws. The concept of law in a democracy is based on reciprocity—the notion that laws must be applied equally to all parties. In a global context, this means that the same rules would apply everywhere in the world without exception. If the world bans nuclear weapons, then no country or group can legally possess them. If global government abolishes war, then nations will have to settle disputes in the world legislature or through the courts. A global government would mandate equal enforcement of global law for all nations, strong or weak.

It is ironic that the US proposed the creation of the League of Nations after WWI and later the creation of the UN at the end of WWII. Even the development of the international Criminal Court began as a US proposal. Yet, in recent times these international institutions have floundered due to a lack of American support.

With the World Federalist Movement in the lead as the convener of a powerful NGO coalition, the United States initially supported the development of the ICC and signed the Rome Statute in 1998 under the Clinton administration. But sadly, on May 6, 2002, the George W. Bush administration nullified this signature, *the first time any country had unsigned a UN treaty*. The Bush administration said it feared an entanglement that could someday be used against the US. Evidently, Bush was more concerned with maintaining maximum power than with promoting international law and human rights.

The US under the Bush administration has continued to dispute or has failed to endorse other antiwar measures. Amazingly, it voted against the land mine treaty ratified by over 130 nations. This treaty was initiated by an American veteran of the Vietnam War who wanted to end the horror of these devices that indiscriminately kill or maim people, long after wars are over.

The US has made little effort in recent years to end nuclear proliferation. It has violated the Anti-Ballistic Missile (ABM) Treaty as well as the Outer Space Treaty. America has not ratified the Comprehensive Nuclear Test Ban Treaty because it wants to develop a tactical mini-nuclear weapon to be used as a bunker-busting bomb. This blurring of the line between nuclear and conventional weapons is a dangerous direction in which to head; it increases the likelihood that nuclear weapons will be used since they will be more like conventional weapons.

The US defense budget consumes roughly half of the US discretionary budget, leaving little money for health care and education. Half of all American scientists and engineers work on military matters. This waste of resources staggers the imagination. This behavior is not a valid defense of a country—it is an offense to the world.

US Fiscal Year 2004 Discretionary Budget Request
($ in Billions)

Military	399
Education	55
Health	49
Justice	34
Housing Assistance	30
Internal Affairs	29
Environment	28
Veterans Benefits	28
Science & Space	24
Transportation	22
Social Services	20
General Government	18
Other Income Security	16
Economic Devel.	14
Soc. Security/Medicare	8
Agriculture	5
Energy	4

Source: Center for Defense Information, CDI.org

The current American administration is obviously not going to lead the world into global governance. But the proposition of this book is that American citizens, in part by harkening back to the ideas of the founders of our republic, *can* become a critical part of the movement for world democracy.

The world community
is standing up to the US

The US militarily dominates the world as the last super-power, but its unilateralist foreign policy is beginning to be challenged by the rest of the world. The best example of this was the early 2003 struggle within the UN Security Council over the US claim that an immediate preemptive invasion of Iraq was needed. The US was forced to argue its case before the UN because, according to the UN Charter, only the Security Council can authorize war. But the Security Council refused to approve the invasion of Iraq.

America's traditional allies France and Germany were especially opposed to the plan to invade. Russia and the Arab League refused support as well. The Bush administration forced an unprecedented split in world opinion that not only pitted the US against its closest allies, but threatened the credibility of the UN itself.

The unilateral invasion of Iraq by Britain and America without UN approval violated the UN Charter, international law, and the US Constitution. The US Constitution states that the US must abide by any treaty ratified by the US Congress. The most important of all such treaties is the UN Charter, which states that no member country shall make war against the government of another country unless it is acting in self-defense. The hubris implied in this unilateral action against Iraq has created new enemies for the United States.

The pretext for the invasion of Iraq was the country's alleged possession of weapons of mass destruction. After finding no weapons of mass destruction, the US and Britain tried to justify the war by stating it was a humanitarian act to remove a brutal dictator. There is, of course, no disputing the fact that Saddam Hussein was a murderous dictator, but for the US and Britain to appoint themselves accuser, judge, jury, and executioner rather than to use and further develop international law is unacceptable. There are many brutal dictators in the world who are ignored because they don't happen to sit on the world's second largest oil reserve.

The fact that the UN would not give its stamp of approval for this invasion was a major victory for the law-abiding countries of the world. Hopefully, the US-British action represented a last gasp of superpower unilateralism in an interdependent world looking for peaceful means to solve disputes and spread democracy. As international law evolves into enforceable global law under a world constitution, the world will respond to genocide, human rights abuse, and tyrants with a single democratic voice and a coordinated military response, with the burden shared by the world as a whole.

The US is currently an obstacle to global environmental protection

The process begun by a UN General Assembly resolution on climate change in 1988 was finalized as a landmark treaty in 1997 in Kyoto, Japan. We noted in an earlier chapter that the Kyoto Protocol, as it has become known, limits the greenhouse gases that countries can produce to 5 percent below 1990 levels. This is to be achieved by developed countries cutting production and giving financial aid to developing countries so that they can cut production of these gases as well. President Clinton agreed to the treaty but his policy, as we have noted, was reversed by President George W. Bush.

The Kyoto Protocol is not perfect—the burden of reducing emissions is not placed equally on all countries—but it is a big first step in a long battle to stop global warming. The European nations had all readily agreed to Kyoto, and they were shocked by President Bush's reluctance to even acknowledge the problem of global warming. Bush nonetheless asserted that the US lifestyle was "not up for negotiation."

We noted earlier that America consumes 25 percent of the world's oil.[10] As the largest consumer of fossil fuel and the largest producer of greenhouse gases, the US has become a pariah in its refusal to sign this important treaty that has been ratified by 120 countries.

Even though the US Environmental Protection Agency has confirmed that global warming is taking place, President Bush dismissed its report as the work of "the bureaucracy."[11] Furthermore, the US government continues to insist on the false assumption that limiting greenhouse gases will have a negative impact on economic activity.

Ironically, the US was once the world leader on the environment. Long ago it created the world's first national park. Beginning in the 1970s, the American government created the Environmental Protection Agency and passed the Clean Air Act, the Clean Water Act, and the Endangered Species Act— legislative actions that set precedents for the entire world. In a world facing dire challenges from global pollution, such as global warming and rainforest destruction, America needs to once again rise to the occasion and show historic leadership.

When a powerful country such as the US imposes its will around the world by force, intimidation, or economic coercion, these counterproductive actions serve to highlight all the more the critical need for one world democracy. A change in US foreign policy to one of demilitarization, concern for the environment, and respect for international law is a necessary first step in building a global government.

The fact remains: America and its citizens are a critical link to world peace and planetary health. The US is now the world's sole military superpower. Americans uniquely have the ability to either continue to block progress or to lead by example and help build a world ruled by law, not force.

America's greatest gift to the world is still its ideas. Today the US needs activists, visionaries, and politicians who understand that the concept of a world ruled by law is the great idea of our age.

> *The US relies very heavily on one card in the international poker game, the military card. We don't like to think of ourselves as a warlike people, but can we expect others to accept us as "peace-loving" when it is really only in arms we trust?*
> —Immanuel Wallerstein

13

How Do Corporations Influence the World?

Bad ideas flourish because they are in the interest of powerful groups.
—Paul Krugman

Our planet is becoming economically one. The battle between communism and capitalism that once divided the world is no longer a major issue in international relations. Global capitalism has had no serious rivals since the breakup of the Soviet Union and the introduction of a market economy in China. The trend toward economic globalization since the collapse of communism is now a unifying force in the world; it is providing the business infrastructure of the coming one world democracy.

In this post-Cold War era, economic ideology no longer plays a large role in determining world affairs. The big players in international politics today are transnational corporations that work in many countries around the globe. Many of these corporations have assets surpassing those of small nations.

But corporations have vastly different agendas from countries—they exist solely to make money; this must be their primary objective if they are to survive in global markets. There is nothing wrong with building corporate wealth, but the unregulated search for maximum short-term profit is often at odds with what is good for the planet over the long term. The purpose of a corporation is to increase the value of its stock, while the sole purpose of government is to promote general welfare—two rather different goals in the scheme of things!

The problem is that while pursuing their private interests, some corporations behave in ways that can lead to widespread human suffering, even on a global scale. Corporations often promote wasteful consumerism. Many create products that are injurious to consumers, such as tobacco, or pursue policies that directly harm the environment or are unfair to labor. Most destructive of all are the corporations that have a stake in the war system—weapons manufacturing and other products and services that support militarism. Weapons manufacturers will need to retool to civilian manufacturing as a democratic world government is formed and the world's people come together to abolish war.

The military-industrial complex unduly influences international relations

Producing and selling arms both domestically and abroad is a highly profitable business. Of course, the US dominates the international arms market, supplying just under half of all arms exports in 2001, roughly 2.5 times more than the second (United Kingdom) and third (Russia) largest suppliers.[1]

We are a long way from the abolition of war, and therefore defense spending is a necessary evil in a world that lacks enforceable global law. But today's aggressive sale of weapons actually fuels the global arms race; each dollar spent makes all of us less secure. The real beneficiaries are none other than the companies that make billions in profits. Defense spending amounts to a transfer of taxpayers' money to global corporations with questionable benefit to the people paying the taxes. The defense industry is dependent on the war system, a system based on fear and the division of the world's people into so-called sovereign nations.

Some weapons systems are not only counterproductive, but egregiously wasteful. For example, the US is scheduled to spend over $60 billion on a missile defense system between 2002 and 2009 that many mainstream experts say will not work and is not actually needed.[2] Amazingly, further development of nuclear weapons systems also continues in the US and other countries that already possess the ability to destroy their adversaries many times over.

No matter how much the US or any other country wastes on systems for defense, this spending can never buy peace— only an uneasy truce until the next war. Real peace comes from *goodwill based on faith in the rule of law*—not from building bigger and better powder kegs in an environment of anarchy.

Corporations keep the irrational war machine in place by constantly lobbying for contracts and laws that favor the production of new weapons. Weapons manufacturers have a vested interest in maintaining the war system as opposed to the more reliable security provided by a system of global law that would eliminate the need for weapons production in the first place.

Large corporations win friends and influence people—with money

The pursuit of their "special interests" by private corporations or individuals, which is their right by law, can also lead them to practices that tempt and eventually corrupt government officials. In some countries, the offenders are drug traffickers who are buying favors or dictators who are amassing personal fortunes. In America, corporations are the main instruments in government corruption. A global government will unfortunately suffer from some degree of corruption and will require the vigilance of its citizens to minimize the influence of special interests over the global public interest.

Corporations can wield their influence on government in two key ways: by directly influencing government officials through lobbying and campaign contributions, and by manipulating how citizens vote through financial control of the mass media.

When corporations donate large sums of money to a presidential or congressional race, they obviously expect favors in return. Such behind-the-scenes manipulation, in combination with voter apathy and a weak media, has resulted in a government that is often for sale to the highest bidder. The largest corporations routinely engage in influence peddling with both political parties; this way, no matter which candidate wins in a given race, they maintain control. But citizens have the ability to win back control over government if they can find the political will to do so. The only thing more powerful than corporate bribery is public outrage in combination with competent, activist, grassroots leadership.

One recent example of outrageous corporate favoritism is the Bush administration's award of a huge contract to Halliburton Corporation for rebuilding Iraq. No other companies were given the chance to bid on this lucrative contract. Meanwhile, Vice President Dick Cheney, who was CEO of Halliburton just prior to coming to office, was receiving deferred compensation from the company of $1 million annually at the time of the contract award.

Another case is the notorious energy bill brought before Congress in 2003. It is widely believed to have been written in large part by the oil companies. The bill was developed in secret meetings with large corporations that were convened by an energy task force chaired by Vice President Cheney, who refused two federal judges' orders to release the minutes from those meetings. Cheney prevailed in the case in an appeal to the US Supreme Court.

Over the last ten years, US corporations have given out more than $1 billion in so-called soft money contributions. This money was no doubt given to gain preferential treatment, with $636 million going to Republicans and $449 million to Democrats.[3]

What sorts of companies are the biggest contributors to the two mainstream parties? According to a survey conducted between 1997 and 1999, number one was Phillip Morris (over $54 million), whose agenda was to make sure the government would continue to allow it to sell tobacco, which kills an estimated 400,000 Americans per year. Number two was Bell Atlantic, now Verizon ($41.9 million), which was fighting antitrust actions because of its many mergers. Number three was ExxonMobil ($34.1 million) whose key interest was to block global warming initiatives and allow drilling in places like the Alaskan Wildlife Refuge. Fourth was Ford Motor Company ($29.5 million), which made a successful effort to hold back fuel regulations, thus allowing an increase in its sales of SUVs. Fifth was Boeing ($26.6 million), which was awarded many Defense Department contracts over that period. And number six was General Motors ($26.3 million), which also lobbied against global warming restrictions and fuel standard improvements. The list of favors goes on and on.[4]

Besides having direct influence over government, corporations also exercise indirect influence over the electorate due to their enormous media presence. The largest corporations control the media through both their ownership stake and their advertising dollars. Numerous studies have demonstrated the media's immense influence over voting and buying behavior.

Over the last twenty years, new laws have led to unprecedented levels of concentration of the ownership of TV, radio, newspapers, magazines, and other media, including cross-ownership in large urban markets. Controversial legislation was proposed recently by the FCC to allow even greater media consolidation, but Congress uncharacteristically found the strength to reject it because of public outcry.

Freedom of the press in America belongs to those who own the press. If one owns a TV or radio station, there are few government restrictions on what can be broadcast. In the past, the FCC's Fairness Doctrine required presentation of opposing views on the airwaves. This wise policy and the rule requiring airtime dedicated to public service have been abolished.

The factor limiting the public's access to alternative points of view is the expense of starting up and then operating a company that is able to compete with billion dollar media giants who work in collusion with government. Gaining access to the media in order to spread an alternative message of a world ruled by law will require creativity and persistence by committed individuals and groups.

Mirroring their growing power in the United States, corporations are also gaining influence worldwide. As developing countries increasingly promote foreign investment, as governments remove restrictions on trade and capital flows through instruments like the World Bank and the WTO, the role of corporations in shaping our world becomes ever larger. If we allow corporations to cross national boundaries in search of profits without any restrictions, the consequences are potentially lethal. But at the same time, the interdependence promoted by multinational corporations presents a unique opportunity for world peace.

Economic globalization cuts both ways

In this era of globalization, stock markets, currencies, and national economies are now interconnected as never before. The size and global reach of corporations has grown enormously in the last thirty years, and the trend is accelerating as giant competitors range the globe in search of profits and higher stock prices. The result has been wrenching changes, with manufacturing jobs migrating to countries with lower labor costs and farmers everywhere being forced to cope in competitive global markets. Many individuals, companies, and even whole countries or regions have been left behind; those with the weakest positions in the world economy have become subject to unregulated exploitation. With few restrictions coming from international institutions, the global environment has also suffered in the process. As this profit-driven trend toward globalization continues to sweep the planet, it is essential that there be a set of rules that levels the playing field between all competitors, standardizes environmental regulations, and ensures workers' rights throughout the world.

In response to the painful effects of globalization, activists around the world have mounted a significant protest movement against global corporations and the treaty organizations that purport to regulate them. These activists are a key constituency of the coming world democracy. As we have noted, this movement of progressive global activists came of age at a large and confrontational demonstration against a meeting of the WTO in 1999 in Seattle, Washington.

This broad citizens' movement is mistakenly thought to be "antiglobal." In reality, it opposes the one-sided policies of transnational corporations and the lack of democratic representation and transparency at organizations that set the rules of international trade (especially the WTO and the World Bank), rather than globalization itself.

In fact, many features of economic globalization have the potential to lead in the direction of world peace. The economic interdependence created by globalized markets makes war less likely. A multinational corporation that has factories and offices in many countries does not want to see those countries at war with each other, potentially destroying the company's property or the infrastructure it needs to bring its products to market. To most multinational corporations, the world is borderless and national frontiers are virtually meaningless—the world is one market.

On the other hand, it should be pointed out that one branch of the corporate world, the military-industrial complex, has a material interest in seeing that the world remains divided against itself.

But the main thrust of the evolution toward an interconnected, capitalistic economic system is progressive. If this system comes under the guidance of democratic global institutions, its dynamism could create a global society that is ripe for the further evolution of global law. But it is essential that corporations have strictly limited influence over the actual development of the global laws that regulate them.

Government needs to control what corporations do; corporations must not control any feature of what government does. Corporations and the capitalist system need regulation for the benefit of society. Individual governments need laws creating a separation of corporations and state. Just as religion must be separated from government in order to have a free society, corporations must be separated from government in order to have an effective democracy. We need to move to a system that satisfies the needs of all, not just the greed of a few. Corporate power must be kept in check at all levels of government: local, national, and global. This is a difficult task, but a crucial one. Progress on this issue is critical if we are to build a peaceful, prosperous, and sustainable world.

As global government evolves, a few things are crucial: The global media must be vigilant and the democratic constituencies represented in the global legislature must be strong enough to keep corporations from having undue influence. At the moment, the deck is stacked very much in favor of transnational corporations. Progressives and people of goodwill must face this challenge, as we move from national to global government. We must do everything possible to ensure that world government serves the needs, not of profit-oriented corporations, but of humanity as a whole.

In the councils of government, we must guard against the acquisition of unwarranted influence, whether sought or unsought, by the military-industrial complex. The potential for the disastrous rise of misplaced power exists and will persist.
—President Dwight D. Eisenhower

Part III

Global Activism
for a New Epoch

14

The Inner Revolution for World Government

The dogmas of the quiet past are inadequate to the stormy present. We must think anew and act anew.
—Abraham Lincoln

Thought precedes action; the outer world is an expression of our inner thoughts and feelings. In this same sense, the new planetary government will be an outer expression of an inner transformation in the hearts and minds of a critical mass of people around the world. To be effective, this critical mass of activists and politicians must have a deep and unwavering commitment to the mission of building one world democracy. Such dedication can only be based on an inner revolution of values and ideals.

This inner transformation starts with an individual's own comprehension of his or her innate status as a world citizen, and the rights and obligations this status implies: the inward realization that all men and women on planet earth are endowed with "the rights of man" that are inherent in the sovereignty of free will. And this freedom is an inalienable gift from "nature's God"—if we may paraphrase Thomas Jefferson.

This transformation of our consciousness also extends to the realization of *planethood*—the intuitive grasp of the collective sovereignty of the peoples of the world. Without exception, the great world religions and humanistic philosophies insist that "we the people are one."

We begin life bonded to one another from the deepest place within us. There is no greater dream than the brotherhood and sisterhood of all humanity arising on the basis of this mysterious bond; our work is to materialize this unity *of* all humankind in a democratic vehicle *for* all humankind.

We are indeed "crusaders for the party of humanity," as Voltaire once put it. We are human beings first, living and dying together on a single planet; only then are we Americans, Russians or Chinese. We thereby affirm our right to be enfranchised as citizens of this world republic—just as our forebears once defended our rights of citizenship in our nations of origin.

Young people are ready for global patriotism

Everywhere it occurs, the propaganda of nationalism and ethnocentrism twists and distorts the inner life of the young. Governments everywhere propound to their young that they should love their country (or race, or ethnicity, or religion) above all others; they preach to soldiers in their teens that it is a high honor to die for the cause. But how different is this from the rhetoric that sent millions of young British, French, and German men into the senseless slaughter in the trenches of WWI?

A century later, we think it safe to say that young people are able to see through this world system. If today's enlightened activists offer them a vision of a world community ruled by law, they will quickly realize that it is a greater honor to be a planetary patriot than a narrow nationalist. They will understand that love of country or ethnicity has a subordinate place in the context of an overriding love for all humanity.

Yet militant nationalism, often a cloak for racism or ethnocentrism, continues to be a driving force behind modern war. Misguided leaders whip up populations into a frenzy—usually based on some illusory fear of an external enemy. Devastating wars are the result. Nationalist and racist propaganda dominated Germany under Hitler, Japan under Hirohito, Serbia under Milosevic, Iraq under Saddam Hussein, and now the United States after the 9/11 attacks. The record is clear: Toxic blends of militarism, racism, and nationalism, often tinged with religious ideology, still lead entire peoples—especially the youth of all countries—to ignore their true interests and follow corrupt leaders into wars of aggression and conquest. This outmoded concept of the militarized nation-state or other subset of humanity is now dissolving and being replaced with the higher concept of world citizenship and global government. We believe these new concepts are spontaneously taking origin in the inner life of activists and leaders, especially the young.

Cultural lines are softening in an interconnected world

The cell phone, satellite television, and the Internet—also the province of the young—have made the planet a more intimate place. Communication technologies and lanes of transportation now connect the world from end to end and top to bottom. International tourism and trade as well as scientific, technical, artistic, athletic, and academic exchanges have vastly increased in recent decades. This unprecedented exchange of cultures and information is leading to the emergence of a *world culture*. Hard cultural lines are softening as interest in other cultures naturally grows through personal contact and media access.

This connectedness forces us to take a personal interest in the fate of the peoples of other nations. For example, huge population increases in developing countries are causing an influx of immigrants to the developed world in search of work or a better life; as a result, most large cities in the West have become showplaces of ethnic diversity. India and China currently have the largest populations and, consequently, send out the greatest numbers of emigrants; more than 400,000 Chinese emigrate each year.[1] On the other hand, thousands of jobs once held by workers in Western countries are now migrating to developing countries in the wake of economic globalization.

Likewise, when the developed world produces greenhouse gases, it triggers floods and hurricanes around the world. And when peasants in Brazil burn off the Amazon rainforests, the atmosphere of the entire globe is affected.

A more ominous example of our interconnectedness is the possibility of a nuclear explosion; the resulting radiation would circle the globe. The terrorist attacks on New York City and Washington, DC, on September 11, 2001, also negatively demonstrated the degree to which the world's people are now interconnected. The whole world joined together in grief for the dead, and for a brief moment the world's people behaved like one family.

World government
will liberate the inner life

According to a famous expression of the eighteenth-century European Enlightenment, "the sleep of reason breeds monsters." Tragically, the absence of global law has bred ideological monsters on the world stage ever since the French Revolution and Napoleon, as many strange new political "isms" and extremist religious ideologies with a political agenda have rushed into the vacuum left behind by the lack of international order and justice. These thought systems filled the "global justice vacuum" by providing their own self-styled version of justice—often based on the hatred of a supposed oppressor or the mischaracterization of an "out group." The thought system of the religious right in the US is one recent example among many.

All such ideologies parasitize off of the injustices of international anarchy. We believe that democratic world government will eventually liberate the world from the worst excesses of these political ideologies and religious beliefs, thus freeing the inner life of the world's people to explore new and more advanced beliefs that are commensurate with the reign of global justice.[2] Global justice based on law is the only reliable solution to international terrorism motivated by political or religious fanaticism, and all other opportunistic systems of vigilante justice.

Separation of "church" and state is needed at the global level

Of course, such a solution requires that the new world government itself be religiously neutral and entirely free of ideologies of hate. The potential for political abuse is greatest when a sectarian ideology or a religion gains power over a sovereign state—and all the more dangerous if it is a world state! The global bill of rights of the new world constitution would guarantee freedom of religion and other human rights already established in international covenants. But the new world government can endorse no religion; world public opinion should strongly discourage international political parties based on religious ideology.

The US Constitution enshrined religious freedom and the separation of church and state for a good reason; the founders were the descendents of emigrants who fled from terrible religious wars in Europe. Because of its long policy of tolerance, the US is now a potpourri of every ethnicity and religion on the face of the earth, all coexisting without violence. A governed world will one day have the same profile.

In countries such as Iran, Israel, and Saudi Arabia, religion plays a large and direct role in government. If such state-sponsored national religions were to promote respect for non-believers, all would be well. But if they teach that outsiders are somehow less worthy, that they must "believe or perish," then this religion is promoting hate and intolerance. Nevertheless, this form of speech would be protected under a universal bill of rights; these misguided leaders only cross the line when they induce their followers to violate global law. In that case, as in all cases under democratic world government, these individual leaders or the perpetrators they inflame would be held individually accountable according to the law.

If indeed it could be proven in a world court that certain religious fanatics carried out the September 11 attacks, then justice would be applied to them and their immediate leaders—rather than entire countries such as Iraq or Afghanistan. If it is true, as many Americans (including fifty percent of New Yorkers according to one professional poll)[3] believe, that the Bush administration was complicit in allowing these attacks to occur, then only those responsible individuals in the US government would stand before the world bar of justice.

A world government would tolerate and protect the freedom of speech and religion of those Jewish fundamentalists who insist that God has forever granted the Jews the entire land of Israel, including the West Bank. However, any form of physical aggression by these believers against the Palestinians or other neighbors would obviously violate global law. The world government would be especially vigilant to make sure that weapons of mass destruction do not fall into the hands of such groups.

Let's consider one more scenario. If a member state of the world federation were to give special treatment to one religion or to a particular race, gender, or ethnic group within their country, this sort of injustice could breed discontent that may spill across national boundaries in such a way as to become a concern for the federation. Obviously, no one wants to be a second-class citizen within their own nation. A world constitution may be designed in such a way as to give affected people legal recourse in global courts against such discrimination within their native countries. After all, they have each been guaranteed basic rights as world citizens according to the global bill of rights. The constitution would also most likely permit the world government to have the power to expel such a country from the federation if it could be proven that its internal laws violate the world constitution's minimum protections of the freedom of speech and religion and against discrimination against citizens within the federation on the basis of race, sex, or ethnicity.

The world democracy movement is the culmination of humankind's long struggle to promote reason and tolerance over suspicion, hatred, and dogma. If political solutions to most injustices can be found, religious fundamentalism will slowly fade away, and religious wars and conflicts will end. The world's people will learn to tolerate each other easily if the rule of global law provides protection from war and predatory corporations, and if the rights of minorities are guaranteed worldwide.

The reasoning and tolerant people of the world will one day form a global government that will guarantee religious freedom while controlling the unlawful excesses of sectarian religions or toxic political ideologies. These leaders will inspire the world with their unshakeable inner commitment to a better world. A new epoch of peace under world law will dawn, rendering issues of basic security and justice a relic of the past. Our planet will then experience a renaissance of the inner life of its world citizens that will manifest in an unprecedented flowering of politics, culture, and spirituality.

For I dipt into the future, far as human eye could see,
saw the vision ofthe world, and all the wonder that
would be; Till the war-drum throbbed nolonger,
and the battle-flags were furl'd, In the Parliament
of man, the Federation of the World.
—Alfred Lord Tennyson

15

Focusing the
Progressive Movement

*The greatest price of refusing to participate
in politics is being governed by your inferiors.*
— Plato

We have argued that world democracy under global law is the best means, and in truth, the *only way* to achieve peace and justice in an interconnected world.

This grand quest for one world democracy is tailor-made for progressives who wish to assert positive and effective leadership in the twenty-first century. It provides for a practical program of transformation that can inspire today's youth and the generations to come. But in order to "get with the program," today's progressives in America and elsewhere must think big—or get out of the way of planetary progress.

This then is our message to mature progressive activists: The generations coming up behind us must face increasingly dire threats to the survival of humanity and of life on earth. Our own generation has responded to these threats with reformism, utopianism, rejectionism, post-modernism, and the single-issue politics of the democratic left. We, the boomer activists, have not yet wrestled with the inexorable need for enforceable global law; we have nearly forgotten the political contributions of the "one world" generation of the late 1940s.

This book retrieves that contribution, and provides a synthesis of the political programs of these two generations of activists. We have named it "enlightened progressivism," but you may call it what you like. As you have seen in this book, this synthesis starts with a radical critique of the toxic world system that is based on the delusion of unlimited national sovereignty, a weak UN, American hegemony, unaccountable global corporations, and unenforceable treaties. We have cautiously pointed to the hidden agenda of global elites who have already formed a shadow world government. We have concluded by proposing a creative program that treats the causes of global dysfunction, not just the symptoms. This prescription offers the solution of democratic global government based on the sovereignty of the world's people, against the false remedy of undemocratic world governance based on the "new world order" of the elites.

Let us bequeath to the next generation our blessing for this quest for genuine global solutions to global problems— democratic world federation. Let us not subject our children and their children to the ravages of an unaccountable new aristocracy whose identity, careers, wealth, and policymaking are based on a cynical adjustment to and manipulation of the current world system.

World federation provides a sweeping vision for the future, one that places all of humanity at its center. Our visionary European cousins have already formed a federal union that has eliminated the threat of war in Europe; so also can America lead the world in forming a federal union on a global scale.

It is a strange fact that, given our globalizing world economy, the Green Party is the only existing political party that is international in scope. If nothing else, the international Green Party's existence in eighty countries around the world is a remarkable foreshadowing of the global political landscape of the future. The day is coming when the world's people will routinely elect representatives to a world legislature. In those great days, there will be numerous global political parties—presumably parties of the left, center, and right. For example, alongside the Green Party might be a Global Labor Party, a Planetary Libertarian Party, or an International Centrist Party.

Today's Green Party stands for UN reform and expansion, for international cooperation and peaceful resolution of conflicts; but it would be a great inspiration if the Greens would be the first to call for the total abolition of war and the immediate creation of a provisional, advisory world legislature—and even for open negotiations to create a global constitution.

Within the progressive wing of the Democratic Party in the US, leadership in providing a vision for global governance has especially been provided by Congressman Dennis Kucinich of Ohio, who among other things used the platform of the presidential election in 2004 to call for a "Department of Peace." The laudable purpose of this institution would be to make nonviolence an organizing principle at home and abroad. But it would be most refreshing if Kucinich and his supporters and allies—including the Progressive Caucus in the Congress and grassroots groups such as the Progressive Democrats of America—would add "the abolition of war through the achievement of enforceable global law" as a key focus of their peace agenda.

In this connection, it should be noted that world federation has been supported in the past by many far-sighted Republicans. In recent times, John B. Anderson, once a

Republican Congressman from Illinois, served for many years as the president of the former World Federalist Association, and John Sutter, a lifelong Republican from Missouri, is serving at the time of writing as president of the Democratic World Federalists based in San Francisco.

Because the US remains the key player in moving toward global law, the political struggle for the great idea of world democracy in the US is critical. Enlightened progressives must think carefully about how to challenge the many entrenched powers and interests in the US that stand in the way of peace, environmental sustainability, and a world ruled by law. Meanwhile, they would do well to join with their allies overseas in building global constituencies for global political parties.

We have also argued that an inner revolution is necessary before this revolution in our global political institutions is possible. Democratic education on a broad scale must take place before we can create a mass audience that is receptive to a world democratic revolution. By the same token, no world government can be viable without a fiercely independent and robust global media that roots out corruption at the global level of governance, while it also reports on the policies and behavior of global political parties.

Obviously, we are far from these ideals today, so how do we bring these ideals down to earth?

The ancient Greek philosophers recognized that a persuasive message requires not just *logos* (a good idea well-argued), but also *ethos* (a respected and credible spokesperson) and *pathos* (a sympathetic and receptive audience). The ancient Greeks knew that great ideas alone are never enough when it comes to statecraft. If Socrates or Plato or Aristotle were alive today, they would surely tell us that the realization of even the grandest of all political ideas—world citizenship, global democracy, and enforceable global law—still requires the development of trustworthy leaders and a sympathetic, open-minded audience if they are to become a reality.

Accordingly, those of us convinced of the intrinsic worth of the idea of one world democracy must first seek out and cultivate powerful spokespeople all over the world, as well as become persuasive leaders ourselves. And second, we must use the world media, educational institutions, and all other means of communication to cultivate the desire for world democracy and global justice in the minds of ordinary people, so that our advocacy for world law can find an increasingly receptive audience.

Allow us to put it this way: In politics, as in other walks of life, it is the stories that spokespeople with *ethos* tell in such a way as to create an environment of *pathos,* that are believed by the ordinary folks at the grassroots. These stories provide the reigning metaphors and symbols that shape politics and consciousness. We need to provide a new story about this planet, and about our place as global citizens on this tiny sphere in space. Through updated stories and metaphors that appeal to the heart as well as the mind, we can change commonly held beliefs about peace, war, and government so that the people of the world will easily come to see that they have a right to govern themselves.

If such steps are taken, we believe that the progressive vanguard of world federation can create the popular will for change, which in turn can be translated into the political will needed to legitimize the creation of a global government through one of the tactical vehicles we have suggested in chapters four and six of this book. In the final analysis, a global government will ultimately be created by people with the power to do so, namely the cultural and political leaders and the elected officials of the world's democratic countries, on the basis of the persistent demand for change by the rightful sovereigns of the planet—the world's people.

We who are committed to one world democracy should know that we are the torchbearers of a great idea, a *logos*. We carry a tremendous responsibility to the future and to all life on earth. Cynics believe nothing will change and so they do nothing; optimists who believe in hope and human potential are the ones who shape the world. Just one person who summons the courage to stand up and speak out against the system of military terror that rules the earth, and for a new system based on law and justice, can give many others the courage to join in. Movements draw strength and energy from such apparently simple actions, each of which occurs one at a time and in apparent isolation. But we never know how one small action might serve as a catalyst to trigger a big response elsewhere. Thus, any ordinary person can provide the hope that shines light into the darkness of people's minds, sending out waves of encouragement and empowerment. The key is to do those things we can do now, with what we have available to us, and then to keep expanding our definition of what can be done.

At the end of World War II, people everywhere were ready to put an end to war. In 1946, the American Institute of Public Opinion asked a representative US sampling, "Do you think the UN Organization should be strengthened to make it a global government with power to control the armed forces of all nations including the United States?" To this question, an astonishing 54 percent answered "yes" and only 22 percent said "no."[1] As amazing as it sounds, it is a fact worth repeating: the majority of Americans polled in 1946, with the horrors of World War II fresh in their minds, were in favor of global government. With courageous activists like Garry Davis in the lead, world federation was a viable idea that inspired a large following all over the world. Unfortunately, this window of opportunity closed with the beginning of the Cold War, which led to the Korean War, which in turn led to all the results we have traced in this book. We know the tragic consequences: humankind has suffered through 170 wars since World War II, with over 25 million people killed. Global warming, terrorism, and nuclear proliferation have become dire threats to humanity's survival.[2] There can be no doubt that we need to get the global government debate going again!

With the Cold War over and with the expansion of the European Union, a new window of opportunity is opening. It has been said that "timing is everything"—and now the time is ripe. Visionary political leadership is now required. An immense amount of work is needed to crack the stranglehold of corporate control of the media so that enlightened progressives can gain access to the general public. It will take creativity, energy, and perseverance to get the message out that another world is possible, and to rally people to the cause of peace and environmental sustainability through global law.

This global governance movement is like the movement that abolished slavery, the women's suffrage movement, the movement for the right to unionize, the civil rights movement, the antiwar movement that helped end the Vietnam War, and other great movements all over the planet that have shaped our world for the better. These movements were composed of ordinary citizens who were told they were powerless and impractical dreamers. Yet they won these rights, triumphing against incredible odds, because they persevered, because they believed in the power of a love that makes anything possible. Yes, we *can* move mountains to create one world democracy under law. It requires abiding hope and the courage to act on our deepest convictions.

> *Few will have the greatness to bend history itself,*
> *but each of us can work to change a small portion*
> *of events and in the total of all those acts will be*
> *written the history of this generation.*
> —Robert F. Kennedy

Appendix A

Key Organizations and Websites in the Global Governance Movement

World Federalist Movement

777 United Nations Plaza, 12th floor
New York, New York 10017
Telephone: (212) 599-1320
Fax: (212) 599-1332
E-mail: wfm@igc.org
http://www.worldfederalist.org

The WFM brings together thirty organizations and 30,000 individual members internationally who "call for an end to the rule of force through a world governed by law, based on strengthened anddemocratized world institutions, [and] inspired by the democratic principles of federalism." The WFM is headquartered across the street from the United Nations in New York City, and is an accredited non-government organization (NGO) through the Economic and Social Council of the UN. It serves as the secretariat for the NGO Coalition for an International Criminal Court, a 1,000+ coalition of civil society organizations.

Citizens for Global Solutions

418 Seventh Street, S.E.
Washington, D.C. 20003-2769
Telephone: (202) 546-3950
Fax: (202) 546-3749
Email: info@globalsolutions.org
http://www.globalsolutions.org

CGS was formed in 2004 out of the merger of the Campaign for UN Reform and the World Federalist Association, two of the largest organizations in the movement for world government in the United States. Today the CGS "envisions a future in which nations work together to abolish war, protect our rights and freedoms, and solve the problems facing humanity that no nation can solve alone. This vision requires effective democratic global institutions that will apply the rule of law while respecting the diversity and autonomy of national and local communities." Now the largest membership organization in the world federalist movement, Citizens for Global Solutions promotes its mission through "member activism and grassroots advocacy, the support of political candidates who share our values, and program initiatives like our International Criminal Court project." CGS's ongoing research is conducted by its "think tank"—the World Federalist Institute.

Democratic World Federalists

55 New Montgomery Street, Room 225
San Francisco, CA 94105-3421
Telephone: (415) 227-4880
Email: wfanca@wfanca.org
http://www.dwfed.org

DWF evolved out of the San Francisco chapter of the World Federalist Association (now the Citizens for Global Solutions) and presents itself as a friendly alternative to the CGS on the question of tactics. In 2004 it became an independently incorporated tax-exempt educational organization, with a large membership in the San Francisco Bay Area, and supporters in fifteen states and three other countries. Its widely read newsletter is *Toward Democratic World Federation.* The Democratic World Federalists indicate an intention to bring to movements for peace, human rights, and social justice the following message: "The citizens of the world are sovereign, and have the right to participate in self-government, delegating their powers at any level they see fit. The United Nations is not a government; and a world government is needed to address the global problems of war, civil conflict, poverty, disease, environmental damage, and to uphold human rights."

The World Constitution and Parliament Association

313 Seventh Avenue
Radford, VA 24141
Fax: (540) 831-5919
Email: govt_rules@yahoo.com
http://www.wcpa.biz
http://www.wcpagren.com
(See also: http://www.worldproblems.net)

WCPA provides logistical support to convene consecutive sessions of what it calls the Provisional World Parliament, and it calls for a Founding Ratification Convention for inaugurating democratic federal world government. The WCPA was responsible for creating the Constitution for the Federation of Earth, a project begun in 1958 and completed in 1991. This so-called Earth Constitution was elaborated by hundreds of people from dozens of countries and all continents. Scrutinized by many international lawyers, scientists and human rights specialists, this model constitution has been translated into twenty-two languages. Eight sessions of Provisional World Parliament have been held, enacting thirty world legislative statutes, which the WCPA says provides a legal basis for democratic world government. The laws promulgated by the Provisional World Parliament "are not subject to approval by national governments, but only subject to the duly-elected world parliament, when that forms. We encourage a Founding Ratification Convention, for at least two dozen national governments to simultaneously ratify the Earth Constitution, thereby providing an impetus for rapid world-wide ratification by both nations and people."

American Movement for World Government

104 Paradise Harbor Blvd, #515
North Palm Beach, FL 33408
Telephone: (561) 863-7187
Fax: (561) 863-5763
http://www.americanmovementforworldgovernment.org

When the (former) World Federalist Association turned its focus
to a more gradualist approach similar to that of the United Nations,
the American Movement for World Government (AMWG) was
established in 1955 to provide an alternative. AMWG created
"a new home for 'all' American world federalists, including those
that favored a constitutional convention." The AMWG recently-
played a significant role in creating the Coalition for Democratic
World Government. It believes that "the growing and unregulated
power of transnational corporations, along with superpower
preemptive unilateral strikes, strongly suggests that NOW is the
time to push for world government." AMWG is associated with
World Peace News (see below).

Association of World Citizens

    55 New Montgomery Street, Suite 224
    San Francisco, CA 94105
    Telephone: (415) 541-9610
    Fax: (650) 745-0640
    Email: info@worldcitizens.org
    http://www.worldcitizens.org

The AWC is "an international peace organization" with branches
in 50 countries. Founded 1975, it has NGO status with the United
Nations and Consultative Status with the UN's Economic and
Social Council. The Association works with "people, progressive
governments, and international institutions to help create a
democratic world community with global governance capable of
maintaining lasting peace and justice through international law.
The key to achieve this goal is for people to think and act as
responsible Citizens of the World." For many years, the AWC
has been a driving force behind the movement for a "people's
assembly" at the United Nations.

The Ashburn Institute/Association to Unite the Democracies

P.O. Box 77164
Washington, D.C. 20013-7164
Telephone; (202) 220-1388
Fax: (202) 220-1389
Email: info@ashburninstitute.org
http://www.ashburninstitute.org

The Ashburn Institute, established in 2004, emerged out of the Association to Unite the Democracies, an organization born in 1939 to promote international peace through the federation of the world's democracies. "We are dedicated to uniting democratic nations, by promoting democracy and cooperation. We do this through educational and cultural exchanges among the representatives of the global community. Greater cooperation and federation will create an environment in which fledging democracies can thrive, and attract other democracies to join. We believe that a federation of democracies is the most effective means to address the common problems of all peoples."

World Service Authority

World Office
1012 14th Street, NW, Suite 205
Washington, D.C. 20005
Telephone: (202) 638-2662
Fax: (202) 638-0638
http://www.worldservice.org

The WSA is the administrative branch of the Government of World Citizens, the organization founded in 1953 by seminal world government activist Garry Davis. In 1949, Davis founded the International Registry of World Citizens; over 750,000 individuals in 150 countries registered at that time, and the number currently registered is about one million. The WSA calls itself "a non-profit, global 'city hall' for individuals everywhere who are seeking to evolve the World Government or are seeking assistance from it." Among the documents available from the WSA is the World Passport, the

World ID Card, and the International Residency Permit. To
date over 2,500,000 WSA passports have been issued. Over 150
countries have recognized the World Passport on a de facto basis.

Coalition for Democratic World Government
http://www.cdwg.org

CDWG is a coalition of many world federalist organizations
"working in various ways toward a civilized system of enforceable
world law." The organization has created a very helpful Consensus
Report based on interviews with thirty-two prominent world
federalists.

United Nations Association
http://www.unausa.org

The United Nations Association of the USA is the nation's largest
grassroots foreign policy organization and the leading center of
policy research on the UN and global issues. UNA-USA offers
the opportunity to connect with issues confronted by the UN
and encourages public support for strong US leadership in the
United Nations. UNA-USA has more than 20,000 active
members in 175 chapters and divisions across the country.

Global Constitution Forum
http://www.globalconstitutionforum.org

The World Federalist Movement - Canada
http://www.worldfederalistscanada.org

Center for War & Peace Studies
http://www.cwps.org

Citizens for a United Earth
http://www.c-u-e.org

Vote World Government
http://www.voteworldgovernment.org

World Beyond Borders
http://worldbeyondborders.org

World Peace News
http://www.worldpeacenews.org

Civitatis International
http://www.civitatis.org

Home Rule Globally
http://home.comcast.net/~home.rule.globally

Consultative Assembly of the People's Congress
http://ascop.editme.com/home

Appendix B

Deck Chairs on the Titanic

By Tad Daley, J.D., Ph.D.

Kofi Annan's *High Level Panel for Change* failed to question the fundamental structure of the sixty-year-old UN Charter.

[Editor's note: This piece first appeared on http://www.alternet.org and http://www.inthenationalinterest.com in Dec 2004 and Jan 2005.]

It is often said incorrectly that the United Nations Charter, framed in San Francisco during the final year of the Second World War, was designed for the world of 1945. It was actually designed for the world of the 1930s. The paramount question on the minds of the Charter's framers, not unreasonably, was "how do we prevent another Adolph Hitler?" The idea at the core of their Charter was that the wartime allies—who became the Security Council's five permanent members—would act in concert to repel all such future aggressions.

But consider the great issues facing the human community six long decades later. Environmental degradation. The AIDS pandemic. Failed states. Intractable poverty. Non-state terrorists. Transnational governance of transnational corporations. Genocides in places remote from great power interests like Darfur and Rwanda. States trying to stem the tide of nuclear proliferation while insisting on retaining vast nuclear arsenals of their own. (It is often forgotten that the Charter was drafted months before the world even learned of the existence of the atomic bomb). Few of these bear much resemblance to Wehrmacht Panzer divisions racing across the Polish border on the first day of September, 1939.

In this context it was greatly disheartening to see the timid and unimaginative report that UN Secretary-General Kofi Annan's High Level Panel for Threats, Challenges, and Change issued on

December 2. The panel did make a number of thoughtful recommendations about criteria for the legitimate use of force in a threat environment radically altered since 1945. But virtually since the UN's inception, those who feel like they didn't get invited to the party have pleaded to make the United Nations more legitimate, more accountable, and more representative of the peoples of the world. Toward this end the panel put forth two slightly varying proposals for expanding the Security Council's membership from fifteen to twenty-four—six seats each for Europe, Africa, Asia, and the Americas. That's it.

The UN's fiftieth anniversary year saw initiatives that proposed a wide range of dramatic changes in the structure of the UN system, like the Commission on Global Governance, the Independent Working Group on the UN in its Second Half Century, the Preferred Futures for the UN symposium, and The South Centre's For a Strong and Democratic UN report—groups brimming with prominent scholars, Nobel laureates and former heads of state. But the High Level Panel said virtually nothing about the dozens of interesting ideas about the democratization of global governance put forth by these groups and others during 1995.

UN reform has never been much a part of the progressive pantheon. It should be now—at least if we believe in basic notions of democratic political participation, and in giving a more direct voice in the affairs of the world to the peoples of the world . . . rather than letting all the decisions be made exclusively by "great power" governments. . . . It seems quite possible that the opportunity for further restructuring may not come again for—who knows? —perhaps another five or six decades. So consider some of the provocative proposals and fundamental questions that were, in the panel's report, conspicuous only by their absence:

♦   Is a small council of "great powers" the only possible mechanism for twenty-first century global governance? Is the San Francisco Charter the only possible kind of UN charter? What kind of UN system would we create if we were designing it from scratch today?

◆ Are we going to be stuck with the results of the Second World War forever until the end of time? What could be more anachronistic than a twenty-first century UN owned and operated by the five winners of a conflict that ended in the first half of the last century?

◆ If the Security Council is going to remain as the primary center of power in the UN, why would a Nigeria or a Brazil, e.g., act to represent African or Latin American interests—as opposed to simply Nigerian or Brazilian interests? After all, no one expects China or France or the United States on the Council today to represent Asian or European or North American interests in any way.

◆ Shouldn't the Arab and Muslim world so central to world politics today have some structural guarantee of permanent representation, rather than just sticking with traditional grade school definitions of geography?

◆ Should there be some kind of democratic legitimacy requirement, so that authoritarian governments that don't "represent" their populations in any meaningful way are not allowed to pretend to do so on the world stage?

◆ How about at least modifying or limiting the veto? Even though it is rarely cast, veto calculations dominate virtually every decision the Security Council makes, because it is always necessary to get all five permanent members on board. To allow a single country to defy the whole rest of the world (e.g., when the vote to retain Boutros Ghali-Ghali as UN Secretary General in 1996 was fourteen-to-one in favor—and the one won) is to perpetuate the single most undemocratic institution in world politics today. (It's often taken as self-evident that the US "would never give up the veto," that is, our ability to prevent the rest of the world from doing something we don't want. But the veto allows other countries to stand in our way too. One can envision the US pursuing an initiative that might garner the support of ten or eleven or even fourteen

Security Council members. But if Russia or China or Britain or France stand opposed, the US is forced to choose between dropping the initiative, or pursuing it without Council authorization and in defiance of international law. This, of course, is precisely what happened in early 2003, when the US abruptly announced that it would drop its efforts to secure a new Security Council resolution authorizing a US invasion of Iraq.)

◆ Is the ineffectual General Assembly, scarcely mentioned in the panel's report, going to remain forever "one nation, one vote, and no power?" How about considering some kind of weighted voting (already used in both the international financial institutions and the EU)? Such a system could take into account not just population, but also financial contributions to the UN and other common international purposes. (Professor Joseph Schwartzberg of the University of Minnesota has performed elaborate mathematical analyses of how various alternative schemes of this kind might operate in practice.) More importantly, how about giving the General Assembly the same kind of power to enact binding international law over at least certain matters that the Security Council now possesses over war and peace matters?

◆ How about a global forum of non-governmental organizations, since national governments are hardly the only international actors in the twenty-first century?

◆ How about a parliamentary assembly, where select national parliamentarians would convene a few times a year in an international forum? Even if only advisory, they would provide a much more direct voice for ordinary citizens on the world stage than executive branch diplomats.

◆ Even better, how about creating a directly elected "People's Assembly" to stand alongside the General Assembly? Professor Richard Falk of Princeton University and Professor Andrew Strauss of Widener University have written about this idea in fora like Foreign Affairs magazine and the International Herald Tribune. Even if only advisory, this body would recognize that just as people in most democracies elect particular individuals to represent them at the local, regional, and national levels, so too might they do so at the global level. And we've already got a directly elected transnational assembly in at least one place—the European Parliament. Such a global people's assembly could open the gates to the emergence of transnational political parties—a historic step forward for democratic political participation.

◆   Can we envision some sort of body that would not just represent parts of the whole, but endeavor to articulate the perspective of the whole, the transnational vital interest, the global public good? George F. Kennan, America's great centenarian sage, has floated the idea of creating some kind of "Global House of Councilors," whose members would represent not any particular state or region, but the welfare of the whole of the human community. They would seek to nurture what the great psychologist Erik Erikson called an "all-human solidarity," what Kennan's Princeton colleague Robert C. Tucker calls an "ethic of specieshood," what Voltaire called "the party of humanity."

Few of these ideas, of course, are politically realistic in the near term. But how can we ever change the political realities of the near term if we don't even discuss what might be desirable in the long term? Couldn't the panel have both made specific recommendations to be considered during the sixtieth anniversary year and put forth some ideas that might be explored further down the road? If politics, as every undergraduate knows, is the art of the possible, shouldn't panels such as this at least try to serve as a catalyst for expanding the parameters of political possibility?

Drive from San Francisco across the Golden Gate Bridge and turn left, and you will arrive before long at John Muir Woods, home of the oldest living things on Planet Earth. Walk along the path back into the forest for a few miles, and you will come across a heavy metal and stone plaque set squarely into the earth. It's dated April 29, 1945—ten days before the surrender of Nazi Germany, more than three months before the atomic devastation of Japan, not yet three weeks since the death of arguably the greatest statesman of the age. The plaque says this: "Here in this grove of enduring redwoods, preserved for posterity, members of the United Nations Conference on International Organizations met on April 29, 1945, to honor the memory of Franklin Delano Roosevelt: Thirty-Second President of the United States, Chief Architect of the United Nations, and Apostle of Lasting Peace for all Mankind."

Get back on the Golden Gate Bridge and cross back into San Francisco, then head East until you get to Washington, DC. Make your way to the Washington Mall and the Jefferson Memorial. There you will find these words: "I am not an advocate for frequent changes in laws and constitutions. But laws and institutions must go hand in hand with the progress of the human mind. . . . We might as well require a man still to wear the coat which fitted him when a boy as civilized society to remain ever under the regimen of their barbarous ancestors."

For those who aspire to lasting peace today, it's time to seek some imaginative new architects. It's time to stop being held hostage by the designs of our barbarous ancestors. It's time to fashion a grown-up coat for the storms of the twenty-first century.

About the author: Tad Daley, who served as Issues and Policy Director for the presidential campaign of Congressman Dennis Kucinich, is Senior Policy Advisor for Progressive Democrats of America.

Appendix C

The World Federalist Movement: A Short History
(With special reference to the role of California)

By Joseph Preston Baratta

[Editor's note: This material is reprinted with permission from a speech originally entitled "California in the History of the World Federalists' Movement." This talk was presented by the author at the annual luncheon of the Democratic World Federalists in San Francisco on April 3, 2005.]

Good afternoon, Ladies and Gentlemen. Greetings under your new name, Democratic World Federalists. I understand that your name change is a response to the abandonment of the name and apparently the ideal by the World Federalist Association, and to the formation of what is called Citizens for Global Solutions.

It is rare for me to have an opportunity to speak before an audience who, I assume, are friendly toward the ideal of a world federation. Our ultimate goal is a world of lasting peace, which means, not the interval between wars, but the presence of justice and liberty, which are the fruits of the rule of law established by government. Federation, then, is the necessary and, we think, practical means to the goal of world peace. In short, it means a constitutionally limited, democratically representative, world federal government, vested with powers by the peoples of the globe and their national governments to enact law reaching to individuals in order to abolish war. To use an old formulation by United World Federalists, "There is no peace without justice, no justice without law, and no law without government."

World federalists saw the *federal* form of world government as the most familiar and practical, since some thirty national federations have been established after the United States, and since a world federation would preserve the historic states while uniting them only for stated purposes, like the maintenance of peace and the regulation of commerce. "Unity and diversity," the motto of United World Federalists, has been the watchword.

I speak with some trepidation, because discussion of international organization or a higher form of government than that of historic states, like the United States of America, touches deep learned and instinctive feelings. I have learned that the idea of world federal government makes many people, not elated, but peculiarly angry. Only the young and those wizened by long experience see it as the hope of the world for permanent peace.

I once spoke to a Rotary Club and assumed that, because Rotary has an active international program, my audience would be interested in UN reform, including involvement by business people. They listened in stony silence and did not even applaud politely when I finished. Only later did I realize the depth of American hostility toward the United Nations. Something similar happened when I once spoke on the enforcement of human rights to a university audience.

So if I should fail to address your concerns, I hope you will make use of the question period following to see if I can really come to grips with what matters to you.

I am a historian of practical, political efforts to establish such a constitutionally limited world federation. I have just published a big book, *The Politics of World Federation* (Praeger, 2004). It comes in two volumes: *United Nations, U.N. Reform, Atomic Control* and *From World Federation to Global Governance.* It is a big book, but it deals with a big subject—the abolition of war by the creation of the rule of world law. The ideal is not too difficult to understand, but the practical achievement through a period of transition is the great difficulty. How do we get from here to there?

I decided that the best way to cast light on this problem was to write a critical, documented history of actual efforts to establish a world federation. The period principally traced is from the collapse of the League of Nations through World War II, to the creation of the United Nations Organization, the first use of atomic bombs, the formation of United World Federalists (UWF), the Cold War, and up to the present—that is, about 1935 to 2002. Readers will find,

I think, that the political conditions, though certainly opposed, were not so very different from those today. I also wished to lay bare the record of the courageous efforts and political ingenuity of the world federalists in order to help those in the future—people like you—to learn from mistakes and to find guidance for what will certainly be a long and fierce struggle. Harris Wofford, the founder of Student Federalists, called it "the revolution to establish politically the brotherhood of man."

G. A. Borgese, the leading spirit of the University of Chicago's Committee to Frame a World Constitution, used to say that a constitution, like his committee's Preliminary Draft of a World Constitution, was a *myth,* in the sense of a "proposal to history," for "a myth incorporates the faith and hope of its age, mediates between the ideal and the real, and calls the mind to action." Similarly, the Constitution of the United States was a proposal to history, as was the Charter of the United Nations. My book is a history of the progress of the myth of a *more perfect* union for the world.

When the Cold War ended—officially in 1990 when President George H. W. Bush, at the signing of the Conventional Forces in Europe Treaty, said the words, "The Cold War is over"—a great historic opportunity opened for rethinking and reorganizing our world. This opportunity may have been squandered, but I think not quite. UN reform is in the air; so is economic globalization. The European Union has just drafted a constitution. Democratic World Federalists have just formed in northern California!

Let me tell you something about California in the world federalist movement. In 1949, the San Francisco chapter of UWF led the most significant effort to pass a state resolution favoring US participation in a world federal government. It was known as the California plan. Some twenty-two states, historically, passed similar resolutions, but most of them were of the Robert Lee Humber or Massachusetts *non-binding* type. What made the California plan significant was that it was a deliberate exercise of Article V of the US Constitution, which provides that when two-thirds of both houses of Congress or two-thirds of the *states* (thirty-two in 1949) propose an amendment, Congress must call a convention to amend the Constitution. Historically, all amendments to the Constitution have been composed by Congress and then submitted to the states, where three–fourths are necessary for ratification. The alternative method, whereby the states take the initiative, has never run to completion, but in some cases Congress has been moved to take up the amendment—most notably in the case of the Seventeenth Amendment providing for the direct election of senators, when twenty-eight of the required thirty-two states had demanded the convention (1912–13). Thus, state resolutions pursuant to Article V would be *binding*.

That was the theory of the California plan. The authors explained that Humber-type resolutions, though they had begun to build political support, "do not necessarily result in educating either the members of the legislature or their constituents, and such resolutions have no real impact at the national level. Their passage has resulted in no legal action, in no concrete step toward world government." A new type of state resolution could both build the movement and advance toward the necessary goal. The authors admitted that world federation "seemed distant" to ordinary members, while action at the state level would give them a "concrete political objective":

> It will provide branches and chapters with a political task of great magnitude, the fulfillment of which will require the sustained effort of large numbers of individual workers. . . . This project contemplates the passage of the resolution only in response to an overwhelming public demand expressed by individual political action and by the action of a wide variety of interested organizations.

The California plan was not undertaken as a lone act of one UWF chapter but as the lead effort in a coordinated, *national plan*. The authors were Philip Amram (Washington), Dean Paul Shipman Andrews (Syracuse Law School), Henry B. Cabot (Boston), Grenville Clark (Dublin, NH), Robert Lee Humber,

Thomas Mahony, Robert C. Rand, Abraham Wilson (counsel to UWF), and others. They conducted a small constitutional debate about this amendment route. Was it necessary? Why? Legally, most admitted the president could negotiate reforms to the UN Charter or even a new world constitution, then present it to the Senate for ratification. "However, for political and psychological reasons," the majority concluded, "it would unquestionably make successful negotiation of the transformation of the UN into world government more likely if our Constitution were amended expressly to grant the President such powers. Such action would dispel all foreign and domestic doubt as to our constitutional capacity, and even more, our political willingness, to enter a world government.

The situation was not unlike that over the necessity of a bill of rights to the federal Constitution during the ratification debates in 1788: Although legally unnecessary, since the people had granted the national government no powers to interfere in their private lives, as a double guarantee and a warning to tyrants, a bill of rights was needed. As other counsel said in the circumstances of 1949, since a world constitution is more than another treaty, "I would doubt the political morality of making so great a change in our form of government without an amendment."

A model binding state resolution was carefully devised. Members were advised to prepare for an aroused opposition. It would be said, for instance, that foreign policy is the business of the President and the State Department, not the states; or that the resolution is an attack on the United Nations; or that it would be dangerous to hold a US constitutional convention, since delegates might not stop at amendments to bring the United States into a world government but attempt to completely overhaul the US government, abolish judicial review, reverse the ruling that corporations are persons, or "other horrible things." The answer to this was that the danger, which did exist, had to be run. In any case, ratification required approval of *three-fourths* of the states. The first state to introduce such a resolution was California.

The California plan, guided by attorney Stanley A. Weigel, accountant Bennet Skewes-Cox, carpenter Carl Broneer, executive director Bob Walker, and California president Alan Cranston (soon to become second UWF president), passed in Sacramento in June 1949. Similar California-type resolutions passed in Maine, New Jersey, North Carolina, Florida, and Connecticut, and they were introduced in ten more states, including Massachusetts.

The legislative struggle in Sacramento was a desperate one, for the proposed resolution was soon perceived as no ordinary bill. I trace the whole story in my book. The political context explains what happened. The California plan was debated at the same time as the Congress of the United States held hearings on some ten world federalist bills, one of which, HCR–64, had attracted 111 cosponsors, including Mike Mansfield, Jacob Javits, Henry Cabot Lodge Jr., Abraham Ribicoff, Christian A. Herter, John F. Kennedy, Gerald Ford, Charles Eaton, Peter Rodino, John M. Vorys, Henry Jackson, and Franklin D. Roosevelt Jr. Its companion in the Senate, SCR–56, attracted twenty-one, including Charles Tobey, Claude Pepper, Hubert Humphrey, Brien McMahon, B. Russell Long, Paul H. Douglas, and Wayne Morse. Senator J. William Fulbright supported a similar bill on European federation, as did Joseph McCarthy. Even Representative Richard Nixon supported a comparable bill known as the ABC plan.

Such activity at state and national levels lifted world federation from an ideal of poets and dreamers to the *political plane.* But at a time of the formation of the North Atlantic Treaty and recognition that the world had entered a Cold War, it provoked intense patriotic opposition, led by the Veterans of Foreign Wars and the Daughters of the American Revolution. The heavy guns of McCarthyism and anticommunism were not yet deployed, yet the VFW and DAR were quite sufficient to snuff out the daring little world federalist movement. Even before the Korean War, which almost everyone, including most UWF leaders, took as proof of the aggressive nature of the Soviet Union and its satellites, the states began to rescind their federalist resolutions. California's was lost by May 1950.

Nevertheless, Stanley Weigel summed up what had been learned:

The Sacramento battleground marked gains of a high order to

UWF of California and UWF nationally. Our relatively new and amateur organization took on the strongest professional and semi-professional political forces in the second largest state of the nation, giving them the fight of their lives. The process brought to light the hidden resources of a band of enlightened men and women genuinely devoted to sound principles, high principles. . . . In the acid test and white heat of a political fight (and what is our mission if it is not political?), . . . champions of UWF have to do too much explaining of a cause which is essentially simple, sound and grounded in American ideals.

To make intelligible this activity of the California world federalists and to bring my story up to the present, I must give you a brief capsule history of the movement. There have been proposals to establish peace by the union of states going back well before Immanuel Kant in *Perpetual Peace* (1795). But all such proposals were not strictly *federalist*. Kant himself, for instance, proposed only a *confederation* of free and independent republics. The League of Nations, established after the Great War in 1919, can be seen as a triumph of the idea of a confederation or association of sovereign states. But after the League began to fail in confrontation with Imperial Japan, Fascist Italy, and Nazi Germany in the 1930s, Clarence Streit, a *New York Times* reporter in Geneva, thought through what would be really necessary to establish peace—a federation of the democracies—and he published the book that started the movement, *Union Now,* in 1939.

Streit calculated that such a union—starting with the Atlantic democracies of the United States, Great Britain, and France—would have a preponderance of power to overawe the fascist states and thus avoid war. But a union was much too difficult to negotiate in the atmosphere of 1939. Nevertheless, in an incident often forgotten, Winston Churchill, in the darkest hour of the defeat of France on 16 June 1940, proposed an Anglo-French union to maintain a joint war against Hitler. This proposal, though rejected by the Paul Reynaud government for fear of the destruction of Paris, nevertheless became the inspiration for Jean Monnet's project to establish the first European Community in 1951.

When the United States was brought into the Second World War in 1941, President Roosevelt formed the Advisory Committee on Post-War Foreign Policy, led effectively by Undersecretary of State Sumner Welles, and that committee drafted the United Nations Charter in secret. As the historian of the committee Harley Notter reports, they considered two alternatives: one, cooperation, as in the discredited League, and two, federation which seemed premature. By the Moscow conference of 1943, it was clear that neither Stalin nor Roosevelt nor Churchill were willing to accept anything stronger than an organization of sovereign states, and the veto provision, protecting the absolute sovereignty of the Big Three (later Five), was tacitly agreed to.

After D-Day in June 1944, Grenville Clark, a great figure in the emerging federalist movement, was sent home by the Secretary of War, Henry Stimson, with the injunction:

> What you should do is go home and try to figure out a way to stop the next war and all future wars. Think of what war will be in twenty-five years. It is intolerable.

Clark then began his work, which led to guidance of United World Federalists and to his and Harvard professor of law Louis B. Sohn's monumental book of systemic UN reform, *World Peace through World Law.*

The Charter of the United Nations was then duly amended, debated, and signed—but with the great power veto intact—in this city of San Francisco in the spring of 1945. The delegates were not aware of the development of atomic bombs. The UN, then, was designed for an old world where nations did not possess nuclear weapons for the conduct of diplomacy and war.

The atomic attacks on Hiroshima and Nagasaki then mobilized the federalists with a desperate sense that, unless nuclear weapons were brought under control by a world government, humanity was doomed in the next general war. The atomic scientists raised the cry, "One World or None!" Mortimer Adler, of the Committee to Draft a World Constitution at the University of

Chicago where the first sustained nuclear reaction was achieved, said that world government could not wait for 500 years but had to be established in *five,* for by 1950, if the Soviet Union acquired the weapon, humanity would be doomed in a nuclear holocaust. Albert Einstein, whose equation $E = mc^2$ had brought the atomic age into existence, emerged as a humane and eloquent champion of the necessity of world government. He once said, "The only way to think of human destiny today is in political terms."

The United States then made in June 1946 a most historic offer to surrender this ultimate weapon to an international Atomic Development Authority. The offer, made in the new UN, was called the Baruch plan. World federalists did not appreciate this plan. They were divided between the popular World Federalists and the more elite Americans United for World Government, and they wasted precious time in rivalries about the ideal through all 1946. So they failed to support the Baruch plan, and even the atomic scientists became dispirited. The plan was a dead letter by December 1946.

The federalists had hardly united in UWF in early 1947 when President Truman announced the new policy of containment of communism, which amounted to a rejection of the ideal of a more perfect union and a reversion to great power politics. The Soviets responded in the fall with the organization of the Cominform. The Cold War began. The pattern of rearmament looked like the beginning of World War III. It only remained "cold" because of mutual fears of nuclear annihilation. The Truman doctrine and Marshall plan were followed by the Czech coup, the introduction of the Deutsche mark by the Berlin blockade, the fall of China by the North Atlantic Treaty. The United States entered into a permanent entangling alliance with Europe.

So the world federalists found themselves united at the worst possible time. The opportunity had been in 1942-43, not 1947-50. The grand alliance of the victorious democracies, liberal and social-ist, as Stalin called his system, had broken up. Federation, as a logical step after the weakness of the UN was revealed in the dawn of atomic energy, became to most people, in the public and the government, simply unthinkable. Nevertheless, world federalists, as in California in 1949, struggled in principled dissent to the rearmament that they regarded as only a temporary solution to the problem of security. Real security lay, they said, in establishing the rule of law.

But UWF had to retreat, perhaps to return to the struggle at another day. In a notorious "top–down decision" of January 1951, Cranston, Cord Meyer, Henry B. Cabot, C. Maxwell Stanley, and the UWF leadership decided to liquidate the field program, fire old chapter organizers like Vernon Nash, discard the tough-minded *World Government News* for a house organ, and concentrate, so they said, on lobbying with top-level officials in the US government. The chapters withered on the vine in the face of VFW slurs on their loyalty. The student movement melted away, never to return. Membership declined from a high of 47,000 to 10,000 and then to 5,000. When the Vietnam War developed, UWF failed to rise to leadership of the antiwar movement, avoiding "political" issues and awaiting the day when all war could be abolished.

The refusal to take on the big issues of war and peace and the consequential loss of *élan* throughout the movement explain the repeated failures to increase membership, take advantage of management studies, raise substantial funds, pass significant legislation, maintain a library or research program, build up a serious journal, merge with SANE, or take on the leadership of the peace movement during the Vietnam War. The ultimate consequence was the loss of UWF's *prestige* within the peace movement. It failed to anticipate and lead effective resistance to the Vietnam War as a practical political step to abolishing all war. The world spirit moved on. UWF itself, worn and weary, collapsed in 1975 (World Federalists, USA, in 1969, was merely a name change), but out of the ashes, like the phoenix, arose under Walter Hoffmann's leadership the World Federalist Association (WFA), a 501(c)3 nonprofit educational organization, and the Campaign for UN Reform (CUNR), a political action committee (1976).

Another name change and apparent abandonment of the unmarketable ideal led to Citizens for Global Solutions in 2004.

What are the lessons of the history of this brave and visionary world federalist movement, which felt the accelerations of history, saw the ultimate necessity of establishing a federal government of the world, yet could not prevail against the politics of nationalism and, now, imperialism? *Atomic fear* has proved an inadequate motivator. People will not be frightened into union. Nationalist politicians will better exploit fear to lead the people back into ready and familiar expedients like military preparedness and a big defense department. What federalists need is a bright, positive vision of peace. People must *love* the idea of a world republic. There is *plenty of time* to think, plan, and work for a better world. "No time!" is the same old argument of atomic fear.

The old battles between the universalists and the Streitists, the democrats and the weighted voting advocates, the minimalists and the maximalists, and the UN reformers and the peoples' convention activists have been resolved. Now there is widespread agreement, even among internationalists who shrink from federalism, in favor of beginning with the liberal democracies, accepting weighted voting of some sort, providing for maximal powers affecting both peace and justice, and working for a transition through gradual UN reform.

A *gradual* approach is best. It is untrue that there is *One World or none!* How did we survive the Cold War? Beware of the poverty of theory. History shows the way. We must preserve the national states as subordinate authorities to a union even as we guide them to unite to enact a common rule of law. UN reform achieved by persuasion is preferable to projects of sudden world revolution.

As Jean Monnet used to say, for the hard work of uniting sovereignties humanity will not act until faced by a *crisis*. Thomas Jefferson said much the same when he wrote, in a famous document, "All experience hath shewn that mankind are more disposed to suffer, while evils are sufferable, than they are to right themselves by changing the forms to which they are accustomed." The world now is faced by a massive crisis, symbolized by the threat of nuclear war, economic depression, ecological collapse, new pandemics, terrorism from the global South, and all the problems of the global *problématique*, beyond the powers of single nations to solve. At the moment, it is only a crisis of the mind. Until there is another disaster on the scale of World War II, demonstrating the failure of the old ways of the sovereign state system, we probably cannot expect great achievement.

There is a large literature now available to guide activists and to hold up as well considered plans. That was lacking in the movement of the 1940s. Two of the best plans are the minimalist World Peace through World Law of Grenville Clark and Louis B. Sohn (1958) and the maximalist Preliminary Draft of a World Constitution of the Chicago committee under Robert M. Hutchins and G.A. Borgese (1948). In Europe, the best model is the Draft Treaty Establishing the European Union of Altiero Spinelli, which passed the European Parliament in 1979 by a vote of 237 to 31 (with forty-three abstentions). If you would know what world federalism means, these are the books to read.

Moreover, there is a large literature in many languages about world federalism. In a survey of mine years ago, I found such works from *seventy-two nations.* Outside of the USA, Canada, and Western Europe, the countries that have produced the most works on world federation are, in this order: India, Japan, and Mexico. It has not been an *American* movement.

The *people* everywhere must become involved in this movement. It is a mistake to think one can have an influence at the top without a mass following. Politicians need to see that the people are ready to undertake the responsibilities of world citizenship no less than to enjoy the benefits. Probably the Declaration of Human Rights needs to be complemented by a declaration of *duties,* as Lucile Green proposed in her *People's Declaration of Human Responsibilities.* Similar declarations of duties were proposed by the delegates to the French National Assembly in 1789 and by the Chicago committee in their draft world constitution in 1948. We need to organize not so much in Washington, as in every city on earth, in Boston and in San Francisco, in order to build the constituency for the national and international changes we contemplate. Democratic World Federalists here in San Francisco is a good sign, as is the Coalition for a Strong UN in Boston.

Federalism has been a movement in the center. The old distinction between left and right, communism and capitalism, is *passé*. The new distinction is between adherents of national sovereignty versus those of the sovereignty of man, the tribe vs. humanity, an anarchy of states vs. world federalism. We *have* happened upon, as Harris Wofford said, humanity's greatest revolution, the revolution to establish politically the brotherhood of man. *Education* will take us only so far; there is no escaping that a movement to unite the family of man is *political*. World federation is not the goal. It is only the *means* to the end. The goal is peace with justice. There are far more models of working federations than the United States of America, or Canada, or Mexico, or Switzerland, or Germany, or Russia, or Nigeria, or Malaysia. As Abraham Lincoln said at the crisis of the American Union, "We must disenthral ourselves." We today are living in a world constitutional crisis. We have entered a period of creative world statesmanship in which the better governed world of the future may look as different from the historic national federations as those federations looked from the confederations and monarchies that preceded them. The European Union may be the best model.

The Bahá'í faith, which developed in Iran after 1844, is the only religion that teaches as a point of doctrine that world peace can practically be achieved by a political union or federal world government. Such a government will abolish war by the familiar instrument of the rule of law, which Bahá'ís call the Lesser Peace. But world federation will provide the minimal political, economic, and social order for the full realization of the potentialities of every human being, that is, for the perfection of religion, which they call the Most Great Peace. We are working for the *Lesser Peace*. Sokka Gakai International of Japan now articulates similar views. When the oneness of humanity is established on a working basis, then the great work of education, science, democratic politics, industry, business enterprise, sport, art, and religion will begin to triumph. World federation achieved by nonviolent agreement will be a long, *long* struggle. We should organize for the long struggle. Remember that the nation state is relatively young, dating it from the Peace of

Westphalia (1648) or from the French Revolution (1789).
International organization is younger, dating it from the
International Telegraphic (now Telecommunications) Union (1865).
World federation is youngest (1939). Its partial realization, European
federation, began to form only in 1951. Those who support this
movement by their efforts or their money should not expect early
success.

The right order of magnitude of what we should do is given
by Grenville Clark's proposal in the early 1950s to establish, with
Ford Foundation money, about a dozen centers for the study of
world law in the principal surviving civilizations on earth. This
proposal was nearly defeated when Secretary of State John Foster
Dulles objected that such centers would interfere with his conduct
of the foreign policy of the United States. But one such center was
established—Robert M. Hutchins' Center for the Study of
Democratic Institutions in Santa Barbara, California. A comparable
measure was Jean Monnet's Action Committee for a United States
of Europe, which drew retired and prospective national premiers like
Guy Mollet and Helmut Schmidt and leaders of major labor unions
and political parties to issue timely, practical proposals leading up to
the Treaty of Rome in 1957.

It is time to reconsider the project, never taken up, of founding a world federalist political party. Like the Republican party in
1856, which aimed to put slavery on a course of ultimate extinction,
a federalist party would aim to make world federal government an
objective of US foreign policy. Such a party would raise up new
leaders, face squarely the necessity of acquiring political power, give
ordinary members something to do, and constrain the movement to
offer the public the whole range of measures antecedent to such an
ultimate political objective. Such a party would have to link up with
similar parties abroad. How else can we achieve *politically* the union
of man?

So, in conclusion, am I hopeful? I am, though my hopes as
I go through life are repeatedly dashed. I have concluded I am an
idealist. As George Santayana said, "An American is an idealist at

work on matter." I love America. I look on this country, formed of immigrants, and see an image of the diverse and well governed world of tomorrow. World federation is *logical*. It stands at the culmination of a long historical progress, as humanity has united larger and larger groups under one government, from the clan to the modern state. It is consistent with the *ideals of the American Revolution,* if we can return those ideals—a "decent respect for the opinions of mankind," and respect for "the Law of Nations"—to the working of our government. "My country, right or wrong," said Carl Schurz at a dark time in 1898. "When right, to be kept right; when wrong to be put right."

I have felt immense joy at finding the historic world federalists, and at tracing their sincere efforts to establish world peace under world law. My method of helping to advance the cause, consistent with the long term, is to write books and to speak like this in order to restore the idea of world federation to *respect* in the academic and public community. For me, politics remains in the future.

I am currently much distressed that President Bush has appointed John Bolton as US ambassador to the UN. Bolton has already said that the United Nations should be reconstituted with the United States as the sole veto power. I welcome the challenge. He is providing the crisis we need. Our alternative is to transform the UN into a representative world republic, on the federal model pioneered by the United States. We propose that it be vested with powers to enact law to solve common global problems and thus inaugurate a just peace.

About the author: Joseph P. Baratta, Ph.D., is the author of *The Politics of World Federation* and an associate professor in the department of history and political science at Worcester State College.

Notes

Introduction

1. Michael Collopy, *Architects of Peace: Visions of Hope in Words and Images*. Novato, CA: New World Library, 2000, p.36.

2. Alan Avert, "The Use of Force, Legitimacy and the UN Charter," *The Interdependent*. Spring 2003, vol. 29, no. 1, p.9.

3. See "The Baruch Plan for World Government" by Peter Myers, 2001; update 2004, http://users.cyberone.com.au/myers/baruch-plan.html.

Chapter 1

1. See *2/15: The Day the World Said No to War*. Oakland, Calif.: AK Press, 2003.

2. See "World Government Web," at http://www.worldservice.org.

Chapter 2

1. See "Reinventing International Institutions," by Tad Daley at http://www.dwfed.org/pp_reinventing.html.

Chapter 4

1. This phrase is quoted from "Ten Ways to Democratize the Global Economy" a useful document produced by the activists at Global Exchange (see http://www.globalexchange.org).

2. See http://www.troydavis.org/writings.html.

3. See Lucile Green, *Journey to a Governed World*. Berkeley, CA: The Uniquest Foundation, 1991.

4. A pictorial history is presented at http://www.worldcitizens.org/awchistory.html.

5. See http://www.sf-pa.org/history.htm.

6. See http://www.worldcitizens.org/awcbranches.html.

7. See Errol Harris, *One World or None: Prescription for Survival.* New Jersey: Humanities Press, 1993, pp 91-108.

8. Some critics of the one world democracy approach suggest that proposals for proportionate representation of the worlds' people could prove dangerous in that cultures at lesser stages of consciousness evolution would gain substantial voting power. But it should be noted that the backward pull of less evolved cultures on the new world polity would be more than compensated for by the wisdom embodied in any global constitution. The US constitution embodied the best ideas of a vanguard of evolved political thinkers whose consciousness levels were far above the residents of the new nation; this scenario can only be expected to be the case with the coming global constitution, that will no doubt (1) feature high standards for membership in the federation, (2) be marked by some sort of "Great Compromise" such as that which led to the model of our bicameral Congress, and (3) include many other offsetting features such as the example of the House of Counselors in the WCPA constitution. But the question of the evolution of culture and "integral theory" remains a crucial one for students of global democracy. In this connection see *A Theory of Everything: An Integral Vision for Business, Politics, Science and Spirituality* by Ken Wilber (Shambhala, 2001) and http://www.ikosmos.com.

9. See Glen Martin, *Century Twenty-One: The Manifesto for Humanity,* Institute on World Problems: Radford, VA, 2003. This document was ratified by the Provisional World Parliament at its seventh session.

10. See Richard Falk and Andrew Strauss, *Nation Magazine,* "Toward a Global Parliament," September 23, 2003, p. 29. It should be noted that the views of Falk and Strauss have evolved as to the best tactical approach to creating a world legislature. At first they were of the opinion that civil society could create the world parliament on its own along with the assistance of some governments who would only play an unofficial supportive role. More recently, as reflected in the *Nation*

Magazine article cited above, they have argued that about twenty to thirty governments would probably be needed to write a treaty to create the body; in this latter approach, the role of civil society would be to campaign to get these governments to assume such a role. Strauss stated in an email to the authors on May 5, 2005 that "relying on a limited number of governments in this way seems to us the more likely approach for a variety of reasons including financial and logistical challenges and the political difficulty of getting civil society to act in a sufficiently unified way to create the parliament. Whichever of the two ways the parliament is created, I think you accurately paraphrase how we believe that it can start from humble origins to become an important global institution."

11. See Richard Falk and Andrew Strauss, "Globalization Needs a Dose of Democracy," in *International Herald Tribune,* October 5, 1999. Also see "Toward Global Parliament," *Foreign Affairs,* January/February 2001 at http://www.foreignaffairs.org/20010101faessay4255/richard-falk-andrew-strauss/toward-global-parliament.html.

12. Falk and Strauss, *Nation Magazine,* op.cit.

13. Falk and Strauss, *Nation Magazine,* op.cit.

14. See Joseph E. Schwartzberg, "Overcoming Practical Difficulties in Creating a World Parliamentary Assembly," in *A Reader on Second Assembly and Parliamentary Proposals.* Saul H. Mendlovitz and Barbara Walker (Editors), Center for UN Reform Education, May 2003, p. 88.

Chapter 5

1. Emery Reves, *The Anatomy of Peace.* New York: Harper & Brothers Publishing, 1945.

Chapter 6

1. The Binding Triad concept was proposed some years ago by Richard Hudson, a journalist who had covered the UN for twenty years. His proposal would amend Article 13 of the United Nations Charter with the purpose of radically altering

the UN's decision-making process. It would enable the UN's General Assembly to make decisions by passing resolutions which become binding as global law when they receive concurrent majority votes based on three factors:
(1) one-nation-one-vote (the same as now)
(2) population
(3) contributions to the UN budget
In other words, a binding world law could be adopted by the General Assembly provided that the law had the support of most of the world's nations, nations representing most of the world's population, and nations representing most of the political/economic/military influence in international affairs. (See http://www.cwps.org for more information)

Chapter 7

1. See "Einstein on Peace and World Government," by Sanderson Beck at http://www.san.beck.org/GPJ23-Einstein.html#1.

2. Helen Caldicott, *The New Nuclear Danger: George W. Bush's Military-Industrial Complex.* New York: The New Press, 2002, p.3.

Chapter 8

1. Christopher Flavin, *State of the World 2002: A Worldwatch Institute Report on Progress Toward a Sustainable Society.* New York: W.W. Norton & Co., 2002, p.130.

2. See Richard Heinberg's *The Party's Over: Oil, War and the Fate of Industrial Societies* (Canada: New Society Publishers, 2003) and Mike Ruppert's *Crossing the Rubicon: The Decline of the American Empire at the End of the Age of Oil* (Canada: New Society Publishers, 2004).

3. See "The Tropical Rainforest" at http://www.geocities.com/dragonhua28/rainforest.htm.

4. For more on population see "World Overpopulation Awareness" at http://www.overpopulation.org.

5. Christopher Flavin, *State of the World 2002: A Worldwatch Institute Report on Progress Toward a Sustainable Society.*

New York: W.W. Norton & Co., 2002.

6. See the UNFPA website:
http://www.unfpa.org/support/friends/34million.htm.

7. See http://www.overpopulation.org.

8. Patricia Reaney, "London Britain has record number of HIV diagnoses in 2002," *Reuters*. Nov. 29, 2002.

9. Gaylord Nelson, *Beyond Earth Day: Fulfilling the Promise*. Madison, Wisconsin: University of Wisconsin Press, 2002, p.48.

10. Jeremy Rifkin, *The Hydrogen Economy*. New York: Jeremy P. Tarcher, 2002, p.5.

11. See "Deaths, Disturbances, Disasters, and Disorders in Chicago" at http://www.chipublib.org/004chicago/disasters/heat_waves.html.

12. Jeremy Rifkin, *The Hydrogen Economy*. New York: Jeremy P. Tarcher, 2002. p.134.

13. See the "Global Greens Charter, Canberra 2001" at http://www.global.greens.org.au/charter.htm.

14. Gaylord Nelson, *Beyond Earth Day: Fulfilling the Promise*. Madison, Wisconsin: University of Wisconsin Press, 2002, p.49.

Chapter 9

1. See "China to Be the World's Second Largest Oil Consumer" at http://test.china.org.cn/english/environment/80145.htm.

Chapter 10

1. Stephanie Strom, "Gates Aims Billions to Attack Illnesses of World's Neediest," in *New York Times,* July 13, 2003.

2. See "Health, Wealth, and Bill Gates," on the *Bill Moyer Show,* PBS, May 9, 2003, http://www.pbs.org.

3. See important alternative views on the causes of 9/11 at http://www.911truth.org and http://www.insidejob-911.com.

Chapter 11

1. See "Current Numbers" by the Center for Immigration Studies at http://www.cis.org/topics/currentnumbers.html.

Chapter 12

1. See http://www.fas.org.

2. See "A Day Without the Pentagon" by the War Resisters League at http://www.warresisters.org/q&a.htm.

3. Clyde Prestowitz, *Rogue Nation: American Unilateralism and the Failure of Good Intentions.* New York: Basic Books, 2003, p.26.

4. Ibid., p.167

5. Ibid., p.168

6. See "Environmentalists Against War," at http://www.EnvirosAgainstWar.org.

7. Richard Heinberg, *The Party's Over: Oil, War and the Fate of Industrial Societies.* Canada: New Society Publishers, 2003.

8. Gaylord Nelson, *Beyond Earth Day: Fulfilling the Promise.* Madison, Wisconsin: University of Wisconsin Press, 2002, p.75.

9. See "Panama: 'Operation Just Cause'—The Human Cost of the US Invasion" by Physicians for Human Rights at http://www.phrusa.org/research/health_effects/humojc.html.

10. See "Environmentalists Against War," at http://www.EnvirosAgainstWar.org.

11. Josie Glausiusz, "A Green Renaissance for the Sahel," in *Discover Magazine,* January 2003, vol.24, no.1, p.66.

Chapter 13

1. See http://www.fas.org.

2. Arianna Huffington, *Pigs at the Trough: How Corporate Greed and Political Corruption Are Undermining America.* New York: Crown Publishers, 2003, p.20.

3. Ibid., p.96. Also, for documentation about trillions of dollars missing from the US Treasury, and collusion of US government officials with the private and corporate insiders who have enriched themselves, see http://whereisthemoney.org.

Chapter 14

1. Christopher Flavin, *State of the World 2002: A Worldwatch Institute Report on Progress Toward a Sustainable Society.* New York: W.W. Norton & Co., 2002, p.131.

2. The Bahá'í religion, which took origin from within Islam in the nineteenth century, is one outstanding example of the kind of advanced religious beliefs that could be considered to be commensurate with a planet governed by enforceable global law. This religion has always promoted progressive social change on a global level, including gender and race equality, universal human rights, and especially democratic world government. Also, unlike many religions, Bahá'ís embrace the findings of science and teach the essential unity of all religions.

   Similar but perhaps even more advanced teachings that may also be considered suitable for the coming epoch of planetary civilization are offered in a lesser-known twentieth century "revelation" called *The Urantia Book,* first published in 1955. (In the text, "Urantia" is purported to be the name of our planet.) Now translated into multiple languages, this unique book presents an eloquent argument for the innate sovereignty of humankind and the need for democratic world government. These teachings are attributed to Jesus Christ as one part of a lengthy section entitled "The Life and Teachings of Jesus." Here for example is one representative excerpt from its critique of national sovereignty: "It is not a question of armaments or disarmament. Neither does the question of conscription or voluntary military service enter into these problems of maintaining world-wide peace. If you take every form of modern mechanical armaments and all types of explosives away from strong nations, they will fight with fists, stones, and clubs as long as they cling to their delusion of the divine right of national sovereignty. War is not man's great and terrible disease; war is a symptom, a result. The real disease is the virus of national sovereignty." [See paper 134, sections 4-6.]

3. See http://www.911truth.org: Findings of a poll by Zogby International showed that half of New Yorkers believe US leaders had foreknowledge of impending 9/11 attacks and "consciously failed" to act.

Chapter 15

1. Greenville Clark and Louis B. Sohn, *World Peace through World Law.* Cambridge, MA: Harvard University Press, 1960.

2. See "A Day Without the Pentagon" by the War Resisters League at http://www.warresisters.org/q&a.htm.

Bibliography

2/15: The Day the World Said No to War. Oakland, CA: A.K. Press/Hello NYC, 2003.

Adler, Mortimer J. *How to Think About War and Peace*. New York: Fordham University Press, 1995.

Barlow, Maude and Tony Clarke. *Global Showdown: How the New Activists Are Fighting Global Corporate Rule*. Toronto: Stoddart Publishing Co., 2002.

Barrata, Joseph. *The Politics of World Federation: United Nations, UN Reform, and Atomic Control*. Westport, CT: Praeger Publishers, 2004.

Caldicott, Helen. *If You Love this Planet*. New York: W.W. Norton & Co., 1992.

————. *The New Nuclear Danger: George W. Bush's Military-Industrial Complex*. New York: The New Press, 2002.

Carter, Richard V. *Survival Meetings: Highlights of the World Government Movement, 1947 to 1952, A Personal Journey*. Lincoln, NB: Writers' Club Press, 2001.

Clark, Greenville and Louis B. Sohn. *World Peace through World Law*. Cambridge, MA: Harvard University Press, 1960.

Clark, Ramsey. *The Fire this Time: U.S. War Crimes in the Gulf*. New York: International Action Center, 2002.

Collopy, Michael. *Architects of Peace: Visions of Hope in Words and Images*. Novato, CA: New World Library, 2000.

Cranston, Alan. *The Sovereignty Revolution*. Palo Alto, CA: Stanford University Press, 2004.

Danaher, Kevin and Jason Mark. *Insurrection: Citizen Challenges to Corporate Power*. New York: Routledge, 2003.

Davis, Garry. *World Government Ready or Not!* Sorentto, ME: Juniper Ledge Publishing Co., 1984.

Derber, Charles. *People Before Profit: The New Globalization in an Age of Terror, Big Money, and Economic Crisis*. New York: St. Martin's Press, 2002.

Doyle, Jack. *Taken for a Ride: Detroit's Big Three and the Politics of Pollution*. New York: Four Walls Eight Windows, 2000.

Dozier, Rush W., Jr. *Why We Hate: Understanding, Curbing and Eliminating Hate in Ourselves and Our World.* New York: Contemporary Books, 2003.

Ehrlich, Paul R. *The Population Explosion.* New York: Touchstone, 1991.

Falk, Richard. *Human Rights Horizons: The Pursuit of Justice in a Globalizing World.* New York: Routledge, 2000.

Falk, Richard, Robert Johansen, and Samuel Kim. *The Constitutional Foundations of World Peace.* New York: State University of New York Press, 1993.

Ferencz, Benjamin B. *New Legal Foundations for Global Survival: Security through the Security Council.* Dobbs Ferry, NY: Oceana Publications, 1994.

Ferencz, Benjamin B. and Ken Keyes, Jr. *Planethood: The Key to Your Future.* Coos Bay, OR: Love Line Book, 1991.

Flavin, Christopher. *State of the World 2002: A Worldwatch Institute Report on Progress Toward a Sustainable Society.* New York: W.W. Norton & Co., 2002.

Frankl, Victor. *Man's Search for Meaning: An Introduction to Logotherapy.* New York: Pocket Books, Simon & Schuster, 1976.

Garrison, Jim. *America As Empire: Global Leader or Rogue Power?* San Francisco, CA: Berrett-Koehler, 2004.

Glossop, Ronald J. *World Federation? A Critical Analysis of Federal World Government.* Jefferson, NC & London: McFarlan & Co., 1993.

Gold, Dore. *Hatred's Kingdom: How Saudi Arabia Supports the New Global Terrorism.* Washington, DC: Regnery Publishing, 2003.

Granstaff, Bill. *Losing Our Democratic Spirit: Congressional Deliberation and the Dictatorship of Propaganda.* Westport, CT: Praeger Publishers, 1999.

Green, Lucile W. *Journey to a Governed World: Through 50 Years in the Peace Movement.* Berkeley, CA: The Uniquest Foundation, 1991.

Harris, Errol E. *One World or None: Prescription for Survival.* New Jersey: Humanities Press, 1993.

Harrison, Paul. *The Third Revolution: Population, Environment and a Sustainable World.* New York: Penguin Books, 1993.

Hartman, Betsy. *Reproductive Rights and Wrongs: The Global Politics of Population Control and Contraceptive Choice.* New York: Harper & Row Publishers, 1987.

Heinberg, Richard. *The Party's Over: Oil, War and the Fate of Industrial Societies.* Canada: New Society Publishers, 2003.

Huffington, Arianna. *Pigs at the Trough: How Corporate Greed and Political Corruption Are Undermining America.* New York: Crown Publishers, 2003.

Inkeles, Ales. *One World Emerging? Convergence and Divergence in Industrial Societies.* Boulder, CO: Westview Press, 1998.

Jonas, Gilbert. *One Shining Moment: A Short History of the American Student World Federalist Movement 1942-1953.* San Jose, CA: iUniverse.com, Inc., 2001.

Kagan, Robert. *Of Paradise and Power: America and Europe in the New World Order.* New York: Random House, 2003.

Kant, Immanuel. *Perpetual Peace and Other Essays.* Indianapolis, IN: Hackett Publishing Co., 1983.

Kimball, Charles. *When Religion Becomes Evil.* New York: HarperCollins, 2002.

Lamont, Carliss. *The Philosophy of Humanism.* Washington, DC: Humanist Press, 2001.

Loeb, Paul Rogat. *Soul of a Citizen: Living with Conviction in a Cynical Time.* New York: St. Martins Press, 1999.

Mailer, Norman. *Why Are We at War?* New York: Random House, 2003.

Martin, Glen. *Century Twenty-One: The Manifesto for Humanity.* Radford, VA: Institute on World Problems, 2003.

Monbiot, George. *A Manifesto for a New World Order.* New York: The New Press, 2004.

Nelson, Gaylord. *Beyond Earth Day: Fulfilling the Promise.* Madison, WI: University of Wisconsin Press, 2002.

Palast, Greg. *The Best Democracy Money Can Buy.* New York: Penguin Group, 2003.

Prestowitz, Clyde. *Rogue Nation: American Unilateralism and the Failure of Good Intentions.* New York: Basic Books, 2003.

Rees, Martin. *Our Final Hour: A Scientist's Warning: How Terror, Error, and Environmental Disaster Threaten Humankind's Future in this Century—On Earth and Beyond.* New York: Basic Books, 2003.

Reeves, Emory. *The Anatomy of Peace.* New York: Harper & Brothers Publishing, 1945.

Reid, T.R. *The United States of Europe: The New Superpower and the End of American Supremacy.* New York: Penguin Press, 2004.

Rifkin, Jeremy. *The Hydrogen Economy: The Creation of the Worldwide Energy Web and the Redistribution of Power on Earth.* New York: Tarcher/Penguin, 2003.

Ruppert, Michael. *Crossing the Rubicon: The Decline of the American Empire at the End of the Age of Oil.* Canada: New Society Publishers, 2004.

Sagan, Carl and Ann Druyan. *Shadows of Forgotten Ancestors.* New York: Ballentine Books, 1993.

Schwartzberg, Joseph E. "Overcoming Practical Difficulties in Creating a World Parliamentary Assembly," in *A Reader on Second Assembly and Parliamentary Proposals.* Saul H. Mendlovitz and Barbara Walker (Eds.), New York: Center for UN Reform Education, May 2003.

Speer, James P. *World Polity: Conflict and War: History, Causes, Consequences, Cures.* Fort Bragg, CA: QED Press, 1986.

The Urantia Book: A Revelation for Humanity. New York: Uversa Press, a subsidiary of Urantia Book Fellowship, 2003.

Walker, Barbara (ed). *Uniting the Peoples and Nations: Readings in World Federalism.* New York: World Federalist Movement, 1994.

Walker, R.B.J. *One World, Many Worlds: Struggles for a Just World Peace.* Boulder, CO: Lynne Rienner Publishers, 1988.

Wells, H.G., ed. by G.P. Wells. *The Last Books of H.G. Wells: The Happy Turning and Mind at the End of its Tether.* London: H.G. Wells Society, 1982.

Wilber, Ken. *A Theory of Everything: An Integral Vision for Business, Politics, Science and Spirituality.* Boston, MA: Shambhala Publications, 2001.

Index

About the Authors

Jerry Tetalman registered as a conscientious objector to the Vietnam War. He is president of the Citizens for Global Solutions of San Diego, and a leading activist in the global government movement. Jerry has an M.A. in psychology, and is a successful businessman dedicated to the pursuit of peace and sustainability. *See:* www.oneworlddemocracy.net.

Byron Belitsos is founder and CEO of Origin Media, Inc., and is publisher of Origin Press. Byron is an author, editor, journalist, and poet, and has been a long-time activist for world federalism. He is a board member of Democratic World Federalists, and was an inaugural member of the Integral Institute.

☐ YES, I want _____ copies of
One World Democracy
at $16 each.

Please add $4.95 shipping for the first book and $1.00 for each additional book. Call for international shipping rates or bulk orders.

CA residents add 7.75% sales tax.

Name _____

Company _____

City _____ State _____ Zip _____

Phone _____

Email _____

Total _____

☐ Check or money order ☐ Visa ☐ Mastercard

Card # _____ Exp. _____

Signature _____

Order by phone: 1.800.247.6553

Order online: originpress.com or oneworlddemocracy.net

Make your check payable and return to:

Origin Press
PO Box 151117
San Rafael, CA 94915